ONLY FOR OUTLIERS & OUTCASTERS: *ENDURING FAMILY*

BY YAMEE

ISBN 978-93-5679-641-6

Publisher: Yamini Krishna Kunduru

First Edition, 2026

Printed by Lightning Source, Inc

Outlier

An outlier is someone who knows they are capable of the impossible, yet remains confused—not because they lack skill, but because they lack direction.

Outcast

An outcast is someone who does not yet know their true potential but dares to attempt the impossible anyway and is mocked by society for trying.

Life is long enough to experience anything and everything you desire.
All you need is the courage to be an outcast and the right guidance to become an outlier.

And this book belongs to both.

The Twins

The Twins burst through the front door, their backpacks swinging wildly as their joyful laughter echoed through the quiet house. They continued their playful chase across the polished living room floor, a whirlwind of energy, until a gentle murmur of voices and the sight of two familiar faces seated on the couch brought their antics to a sudden, skidding halt.

Grandmother's eyes twinkled, and Grandfather leaned forward with a gentle smile, hands resting on his knees. Though the Twins had seen them many times before, the moment felt as new as ever. The Twins froze, exchanging wide-eyed glances, before Taizer buried his face in his mother's dress, and Tara hid behind her father's comforting embrace.

Their shyness met with quiet chuckles.

"Still the same," Grandmother whispered with enduring fondness. "Every time, it's as if they're meeting us for the very first time."

From behind their parents, Taizer and Tara curiously peeked out, watching and waiting. The warmth of family gently drew them forward, straight into the loving arms of their grandparents. Taizer and Tara's excitement only grew, knowing they had more people to shower them with attention at home, and their irresistible cuteness instantly charmed their grandparents.

Taizer and Tara were about to turn eleven, and their parents were busy planning a birthday party for the upcoming weekend, so the grandparents arrived early to help with the preparations.

By the weekend, the house was buzzing with excitement—a vibrant mix of joy, friends, neighbors, and relatives, all gathered to celebrate the Twins' special day at a warm, intimate party. As is often the case, the adults tried to engage the Twins with playful chatter, but the children, as they do, happily ignored most of the grown-ups. Breaking through the noise, one guest asked the inevitable, age-old adult question. "What do you want to be when you grow up?"

The Twins were quick to answer. Taizer said, "I want to be a cop," while his sibling Tara declared, "I want to be a doctor."

Their relatives and friends merely laughed, accustomed to the Twins' annually changing ambitions. Last year, they wanted to be a teacher and a chef. The year before that, it was a superhero and a lawyer.

After the party, everyone was so tired, but the Twins were still buzzing with sugar cake rush energy, desperate to keep the celebration alive; their energy was a stark contrast to the adults' fatigue. Their mother and grandmother, after a considerable struggle, finally managed to coax them upstairs and tucked them into bed, while the men stayed downstairs to help clean up. Once they believed the children were finally asleep, the mother and grandmother settled into a hushed conversation. They reflected on how well the party had gone and chuckled at Taizer's unexpected answer about wanting to be a police officer. Later, they dismissed it, speculating that Taizer might have drawn inspiration from the animated shows he had been watching recently. "Of course, Taizer is the first-bencher, always keen to learn and so good at studies," they joked. And Tara? She's the last-bencher, the one who just wants to become a chef." They laughed it off while exchanging a knowing glance, a mixture of amusement and deep affection for their very different children.

Their words actually carried some truth. The Twins were strikingly different: Taizer was always active, curious, and eager to learn, while Tara would find reasons to avoid studies. Since childhood, she would get grumpy whenever she was asked to do homework or even open books.

The twins' parents, though, were both easygoing, taking the "go with the flow" quote seriously, never forcing studies on either of them. One excelled naturally, while the other simply did enough to just barely get by.

Taizer was highly competitive, often in tears, even when he felt he didn't achieve the results he deserved. Tara, on the other hand, was content with whatever grades came by, unbothered and carefree. Watching how differently the Twins reacted to their grades often left their parents in awe. No matter how differently they were doing in school, they never let their differences come between them. They were so playful and creative, inventing new games with their parents.

But the but came by. Something shifted right after the birthday party. From the very next morning, Taizer began behaving oddly with his twin sister, Tara. He even left for school without even waiting for her. Their father has to drop Tara off separately. That evening, the two returned home apart as well, something that had never happened before. During homework time in their evening study hours, Taizer began belittling his twin sister whenever she asked for help, pointing at her low scores. What started one day became a routine, and guilt-tripping his twin sister became almost a habit. No matter how often their parents tried to stop and correct him, he would only listen to them then and there and shrug it off later.

Tara, however, never let go of her affection towards her twin brother. She is always making every effort to be close to him. She even got ready so early so she could walk with him to school, and even in the evenings, she rushed to the gate after the last bell just to be by his side.

This went on for some time until one day the twins' favorite grandmother stepped in. She sat down with Taizer and gently asked why he was avoiding his sister and constantly making her feel guilty about her studies.

Taizer burst into tears like never before. He confessed that his friends, especially Taksh, have been teasing him and making fun of him because of Tara. No matter how high his ranks were, they always dragged him down by laughing about Tara's low scores.

"Even at the birthday party," he sobbed, "they mocked her when she said she wanted to become a doctor. 'How can she be a doctor when she has the lowest grades in the whole school?' they jeered."

His parents and grandmother exchanged knowing glances when suddenly it all made sense. This is why Taizer never listened when they asked him to stop guilt-tripping his sister. He did care for her, but his friends had turned her weakness into his shame. And in trying to defend himself against their taunts, Taizer had let ego creep into his sibling care.

Yet, the family also understood why Tara had stayed calm and loving through it all, knowing that one of the twins, Tara, had been deaf since birth. She couldn't hear the sting in her brother's voice or the sharpness of his words. But all she could sense was her brother urging her to improve her studies, which she genuinely is trying to do.

The irony is, Taizer had seen his twin sister Tara struggle from the start with her hearing. But instead of protecting her from the world's harshness, he had let that harshness seep into his heart. Taizer, blinded by his wounded pride, couldn't see his twin's progress and forgot the bond they shared. All he could feel was the weight of his friends' voices, drawing out the truth right in front of him—a bond that was meant to lift each other, not pull each other down.

Even the family did not know how to convince eleven-year-old Taizer that family bonding should be stronger than ego. That his relationship with his twin sister should matter more than ranks or the voices of outsiders. These are basic truths even grown-ups sometimes struggle to hold on to. So instead of lecturing, they chose silence and gentleness. His grandmother stroked his hair, his mother held his hand, and his father said, "Taizer, we know it hurts. But don't let the world make you forget who your sister is to you." They didn't have the perfect words. They didn't know how to teach the balance between competition and compassion to the twins. All they could hope for was that, in time, Taizer himself would discover it, because siblings usually manage to remember how much they care about each other.

Beliefs

After Taizer allowed differences to come between him and his sister, two natural questions arise for us to ponder:

1. Is ego so powerful that it blinds us to affection, just as it did for Taizer when he tried to hurt his own beloved sister?

2. How did Tara remain unaffected by her brother's ego, continuing to express affection despite his sound rage?

Taizer's life is overflowing with love: he has caring parents and an affectionate sister and is a rank holder in school. And yet, he still ended up hurting the person dearest to him.

Just like many of us, Taizer was trapped by one powerful root of emotion: Fear. Fear of not fitting in. Fear of being laughed at. Fear of appearing different from the crowd.

Since birth, the world around us has taught us everything. How to walk, how to talk, what and how to study, and how to behave—a system of "this is how it should be" script is placed right in front of us, and *we* are told to follow it step by step. And falling out of these steps often brings the fear of not fitting in.

So, when Taizer's friends mocked him because of his sister, something cracked in his pure child's heart. No matter how well he performed, their laughter made him feel "less." He began to see his sister not as his companion but as the reason for his shame. His pure sibling affection became clouded by ego—a defense born from fear, saying, "Protect yourself. Don't let them see your weakness." So instead of standing by his sister, Taizer tried to distance himself from his weakness, which he perceived as his sister. Instead of protecting her, he joined the voices that mocked her, because in his young mind, it felt safer to stand with the crowd than to stand apart.

And isn't that what happens to many of us? Surrounded by love, comfort, and blessings, we still hurt ourselves or those dearest to us because fear of not fitting in whispers, "You are not enough unless you match the world's measuring scale."

And the measuring scale we are given is

School → College → Career → Money → Home → Marriage → Travel → Kids

I am not against this measuring tape or this process. In fact, I believe it helps each and every one of us discover ourselves step by step in this whole life journey. Because, to be honest, none of us are born with a manual, so following such a process is not at all wrong.

The mistake lies in thinking—or, worse, in making others believe—that it is the only way to live a life. That mistake is exactly what we keep forcing on each other—the belief that life must follow one fixed script.

If someone struggles in school, or stumbles in their career, or chooses not to marry or have kids, some of us even try to rewrite the given script by falling in love first and settling down later, as if shuffling the order of the same steps is still the only choice—even then society is quick to label them with names like failure, or not worth it. Making everyone believe this script with a measuring tape is the only way to live a life is the root cause of all human problems. I repeat: All.

Because when even the slightest misalignment happens in this process of "looking alike," we humans are branded as failures. And in chasing this sameness, we have all forgotten the actual truth:

We human beings are born with free will—with freedom.

Like the old example of a bird caged since birth, it might forget that it was born with wings. In the same way, you may have also forgotten that you were born with free will, with the complete ability to be whatever you wish, in whichever way you wish. But there's a condition: you must remain responsible to yourself, your actions, your family, and the society you are part of.

Belief—it is something that is accepted, considered to be true, or held as an opinion. - *Google's Dictionary Definition.*

A belief is born in isolation. It begins as a thought in the mind of one person and then spreads across many like-minded people. Once enough of us agree, that thought hardens into a "truth" for that group. That is how a belief is formed and spread.

Here comes another simple question for you: are all humans alike? Are we all the same?

Of course not. Since birth, every single one of us carries different circumstances, different personalities, and different thought patterns formed based on those circumstances and personalities. We may share the basic human functions—eating, sleeping, and breathing—but beyond that, every human being is as unique as your fingerprints.

And this is where fear begins. When one person's thought becomes a belief, and that belief is forced upon everyone else as the only way to live, it crushes the courage to be unique.

For example, take the lion in the forest. For some people, the lion is ruthless, a creature that kills innocent animals whenever it feels hungry. From their perspective, the lion is cruel, destructive, and a threat to life. Perhaps this is the opinion of someone who has been a vegetarian since birth. That is their circumstance since birth, which turned into their belief.

But for some others, the same lion is a savior. By hunting plant-eating animals, it protects the balance of the forest. It saves trees and plants from overgrazing, preventing deforestation. From their perspective, the lion is not a villain but a guardian. This belief may come from someone who has seen how balance in nature is maintained firsthand, or perhaps they might have been saved from danger by the least expected person when they needed it the most. Again, that is their circumstance that formed their belief.

The Lion is the same in both cases. For one, it is the villain; for others, it is the hero. What changes is the lens through which it is seen. Do you now see how a person builds beliefs? Beliefs are not born out of thin air, nor handed down from the sky. They are built piece by piece, purely based on the circumstances and experiences given to you since birth. What you see, what you hear, what you are taught, what you suffer, and what you enjoy—all of these moments stack together to form the lens through which you look at the world.

That lens is your perspective, and when it hardens, it becomes a belief. And just as no two people live the exact same life, no two perspectives can ever be identical. Which means, naturally, there will always be multiple perspectives for everything.

These beliefs in our lives can be formed in two ways: by the self and by external influences.

Basically, there are two main types of beliefs: Internal and External.

1. Internal Beliefs

These are the beliefs born purely from your self-experiences. They are not formed by listening to someone, nor by being taught, but by directly experiencing something with all your five senses—sight, hearing, smell, taste, and touch.

Think about this: A child who eats a lemon by mistake and finds it unbearably sour will avoid lemons in the future. That belief—*lemons are unpleasant*—was born from a direct taste experience. No external validation was needed. Similarly, the same child who eats ice cream and feels delight will crave it again. That belief—*ice cream is good*—also came from a direct taste experience.

2. External Beliefs

Now, these are the beliefs formed mostly by guidance or influence from outside sources—your parents, teachers, friends, or society. They come to you through instruction, culture, or authority, rather than through your personal sense experience.

For example, that same child who found the lemon sour may later be told by parents or teachers that lemons are healthy and good for the body. This external instruction has the potential to contradict the child's internal belief. Similarly, even though the child craves ice cream, they may be told that it's bad for their health and should be avoided.

To simply put:
Internal beliefs are pure self-experiences. You first feel them with one or the other of the five senses, and only later do you build words to describe them, or sometimes the experience becomes indescribable.

External beliefs are taught to you. They are first taught to you in words, and only later do you try to experience them.

As human beings, we naturally follow both. Sometimes we lean on internal beliefs. Sometimes on external ones. And often, we live with a mix of both.

Have you observed how easy it is for parents or teachers to change an internal belief?

Take our earlier example: a child eats ice cream and feels joy; an internal belief is formed: *ice cream is wonderful*. However, with just a few words, such as "ice cream is bad for your health," parents or teachers gradually replaced the child's internal belief with their own external belief. The child may resist at first, but eventually, the external belief starts to overpower the internal one.

But now, let's look at the opposite case:

What happens when you try to change an external belief using your internal experience?

Consider Taizer's situation. His internal belief, "My sister is my family," was being crushed by an external belief forced upon him by friends—"Your sister cannot become a doctor; she is a low performer at school." At home, his internal experience was pure affection, laughter, and bonding. But outside, the external words of society echoed louder: grades defined worth, and intelligence defined value. His friends mocked him, and those external beliefs planted the seed of confusion/doubt in his mind.

And when doubt entered, fear followed. When fear entered, ego rose. And when the ego rose, affection was blinded.

And this takes us back to our very first question: **Is ego so powerful that it blinds humanity, just like it did with Taizer, who tried to hurt his beloved sister?**

Love, by nature, is selfless. Ego, by nature, is self-centered. When ego dominates, you stop seeing people as they are and start seeing them only in relation to your benefits. Taizer didn't stop caring for his sister, but he stopped expressing that care because his ego made her look like a threat to his identity in front of others.

Taizer was taught in school that external grades were the stepping stones to success, the ticket to great heights. At home, he lived and breathed the warmth of internal sibling affection. And in between, his friends bullied him about his sister's performance at school.

Now here lies the conflict, and this is where it gets complicated: both beliefs are true in their own way. Yes, grades do matter in school, and yes, his sibling bond is real. But when the two truths collided, confusion was born.

As humans, by nature, we tend to trust external beliefs over internal ones because external beliefs come with proof and majority support. They are validated by society.

Whereas internal beliefs, on the other hand, are invisible, personal, and often impossible to prove—they are simply the self-sensed experience.

Taizer couldn't argue with his friends: "She is my sister, and that's more than enough." If he did, he feared risking his so-called "social connection." That was his first step into fear. Fear of being left out pushed him to avoid his sister. He wanted to maintain his image as a topper and class leader. He needed his votes in school, his social approval.

And as humans, we are interdependent. Even the most introverted among us rely on others. The food we eat, the clothes we wear, and the tools we use are all creations of collective living. Naturally, in our lives, survival depends on social ties.

But deep down, Taizer knew he was not being himself. The freedom to care for his sister, to be his true self, was disrupted. And that inner conflict, that gap between who he was and how he is acting now, became his frustration.

So this answers a crucial question for us. **What happens when you try to change an external belief using your internal experience?**

Changing an internal belief with an external one is quite simple, provided you have proper proof and solid external support. But here is the real issue: when you try to mess with deep-seated external beliefs using your personal internal experience, it causes serious psychological and social conflict. When a personal, lived experience contradicts something everyone believes, your internal feeling simply doesn't have the necessary social weight to change that established external belief. This conflict mainly provides two results:

1. **Fear of being an outcast:** Challenging the external belief means risking social boycott. This fear of being labelled an outcast often leads to keeping silent in public or just pretending to agree with the external belief, hiding the real, true internal feeling.

2. **Psychological Tension:** Confusion, frustration, maybe even depression (because you can't fully live by your internal conviction but can't give 100% to the external either): this is basically emotional gridlock. The internal belief pulls you one way, while the external one pulls you the other way. This leads to:

- **Frustration**: You feel this when you can't reconcile your two truths or make the external world accept your internal truth.

- **Confusion**: You lack clarity about which belief is more real or more important, leading to paralysis in making decisions.

- **Depression/Anxiety**: This is a deep sense of despair or unease arising from the continuous, taxing effort of maintaining two parallel, contradictory narratives—the public one and the private one. You cannot fully commit to your internal conviction (because of the social cost), and you cannot fully embody the external one (because it feels false), leading to a state of profound alienation and arrested development.

It becomes a constant "this or that" phase.

Because internal beliefs often lack proof and majority votes, most of us unknowingly tend to sacrifice them. On the contrary, external beliefs are so loud, so repetitive, that we stop noticing the subtle truths born from our own self-sense experiences.

Now, there are also times when some people swing the other way, leaning completely on internal beliefs and ignoring the external ones. But both extremes come with risks. Every internal belief can be good or bad. And similarly, every external belief can also be right or wrong.

Think about this example: When Tara and Taizer were learning how to ride a bicycle, both fell and felt pain. Their parents encouraged them, saying, "It's okay, try again." Taizer heard those external voices and chose to ignore his painful internal experience. Slowly, he overcame the fear of pain and mastered cycling. But Tara, being deaf since birth, couldn't receive that external encouragement. She trusted only her internal experience of pain. This made her avoid cycling altogether and carry a fear of it.

In the same way, if someone forms an internal belief that they can fly with their hands, you know it is dangerous to them. On the other hand, blindly obeying external beliefs without question can also suffocate your individuality and freedom.

So, as humans, our real responsibility is balance. We cannot simply do whatever we feel internally, nor can we blindly accept whatever is taught externally. A clean conscious balance is required.

That clean conscious balance of internal vs. external belief can only be achieved by knowing the difference between what is right and what is wrong.

Because both internal and external beliefs have the potential to mislead us.

- Internal beliefs come from direct sense experience, but experience alone can be dangerous, like speeding through traffic can be thrilling internally but is harmful.

- External beliefs come from majority voices, but the crowd is not always right. History is filled with examples where society declared something "true" that was later proven false.

So how do you decide which belief to hold on to?

By passing it through a simple filter: Right and Wrong.

There is Right, and There is Wrong.

Taizer grew up in an environment filled with love. His parents believed in guidance, not force. They offered him a clear path, but the choice to follow it—at his own speed—was entirely his. With that freedom, Taizer naturally excelled at studies. For him, learning felt like discovery, and excellent grades were simply a reward for his effort. However, the external beliefs led him to think differently.

Now consider his twin, Tara. She grew up in the exact same environment, with the same love and freedom. But studies didn't click for her. And this is where their parents made a critical choice: instead of forcing her into Taizer's mold, they encouraged her to explore other things, where her imagination thrived to find out where her heart found joy. Her worth was never tied to a score on a paper; it was tied to the exploration of her unique self.

Then we come to Taksh, Taizer's best friend. Taksh lived in a different world entirely. In his house, love, and you could say, 'freedom,' were offered only in the form of control. For Taksh, love meant proving himself, earning good grades, and securing ranks. If he fell behind, he was pushed into extra classes, with no freedom to try or explore anything else. For Taksh, studies weren't a path to growth. They were the only rule of survival, the only door to being valued at home.

We can clearly see three distinct children here. They're living under three very different personal skies.

- For Taizer, grades were a reward—a prize for his effort.

- For Tara, grades were utterly irrelevant; she was busy exploring the world and herself.

- For Taksh, grades became a crushing measure of his entire self-worth.

Yet, in school, all three were placed under the exact same system. And within that system, grades were elevated to an external belief, a universal yardstick to measure who was 'good' and who was 'bad.' That external, imposed belief is the very root cause of the bullying.

So, when Taizer, one of the twins, achieved a higher rank than Taksh right before their twin's birthday week, his friend Taksh felt an immediate, devastating loss. His rank wasn't just a number; it was tied to the very affection he received at home. Taksh's parents' love seemed to shrink, contingent upon his performance.

Now, consider Tara. She moved through the world with an utter disregard for grades, laughing and playing, living entirely within her own rhythm. To Taksh, wounded and desperate for validation, her freedom was incomprehensible. It was, in fact, the very opposite of what he believed gave life worth. Out of this profound pain, his frustration became an outward weapon, targeting both Taizer and Tara at the birthday party. Tara's very existence, her carefree nature, threatened the core belief he had been taught: that his worth is measured by his rank.

That pain, that anger, was so contagious that Taksh's fear and his belief system—that love is conditional—leapt into Taizer's heart.

Taizer, the boy who had only ever known the certainty of unconditional love and freedom, now experienced fear for the first time. *"What if my friends don't respect me because of Tara? What if her grades pull me down too?"*

This sudden, corrosive thought clouded his pure sibling affection for his sister. And so, he began to avoid her, mock her genuine doubts, and carry a weight—a belief system—that he didn't even understand. This is how the fear of conditional love spreads.

Now, how do you break these contagious beliefs that might be bad/wrong?

By being like Tara.

Tara saw her brother's rage, but she didn't let it define him. She felt his avoidance, but she didn't stop waiting at the school gate after school. She heard with her heart what her ears could not: his care, hidden beneath the noise of ego.

Just like Taizer, Tara, too, felt that internal sibling affection. But how was she able not to let the noise of ego inside her?

This answers our second question—**How did Tara remain unaffected by her brother's ego while still caring for him despite his intense rage?**

Perhaps, in part, it was because she is deaf. She was lucky enough not to hear the loud external voices about grades, ranks, or confusion. But there was something even deeper guiding her, something more powerful than silence.

And what was that? That is: Tara valued Intention.

Think about it. She didn't take her brother's harsh words at face value. She searched for the root, the *why*. And what she saw was not cruelty, but concern. Taizer wanted her to improve, to do well. He didn't want her to be laughed at. We know his way of expressing was hurtful—that's because he himself was confused and hurt by Taksh—but his intention, at its core, was still affection, albeit confused.

This leads us to a crucial point. Intention is what decides if something is good or bad, right or wrong.

Every thought, every desire, every action you take—all of them sprout from a single root: Intention.

Take the case of Tara. She knew her brother's intention was not to break her spirit but to push her forward, even if it looked clumsy and confused. So she didn't mirror his anger. Instead, she mirrored his hidden care back to him through patience, forgiveness, and affection.

Now, consider Taizer's friend, Taksh. His parents seemed controlling, always strict about studies, limiting his freedom. At first glance, you might think it looks like pure selfishness of parents, forcing their child into a mold. But if you look deeper, the root intention was actually a good one. They wanted him to do better in life, to sharpen his gifts, and to unlock his potential.

Here's the truth of the matter: Taksh was naturally talented. He could score very well even with just an hour of focus. But he was lazy, easily distracted by cartoons and games. His parents knew this and tightened the reins. Their strictness was not to destroy his joy but to guide him towards discipline. In a way, it was a form of good intention. Both Taksh and his parents will benefit from that good intention.

When an intention comes from a place of love, empathy, and shared growth, when the intention helps you grow without harming or suppressing others, that's what makes an intention right or good.

But when an intention serves only the self at the cost of someone else's peace or dignity, that is when an intention is wrong or bad.

We live in a connected world. So whatever you do affects not just yourself, but also your relationships, your family, and even society too. Therefore, it is your responsibility to distinguish between good and bad intentions.

Let's look at Taksh. Instead of seeing his parents' intention, his ego latched onto the restriction of his favorite cartoons. He himself tied his self-worth to grades.

And here is where Taksh's intention turned unhealthy. Taksh's parents' intention remained healthy, but his own heart grew cloudy with an unhealthy intention called jealousy.

That jealousy spilled over into bullying Taizer and mocking Tara. This was no longer about grades anymore; it was about dragging someone else down so the bully could feel taller. That's a bad intention rooted in jealousy, preventing growth and benefiting no one.

Now, consider this: When you make a choice that might feel uncomfortable for others in the short term, but it's rooted in love and vision, and when it is done with honesty, respect, and shared purpose, in time, everyone benefits. That's a good intention.

For example, when a mother is strict with her child, it may seem harsh to an outsider at first. But she intends to help the child grow into a better person. In the end, it benefits both the child and the mother—and even society. I call that healthy selfishness.

When our actions only benefit us and deeply hurt others,

emotionally or physically, this kind of intention comes from a bad place, and it usually leads to more problems down the line.

For example, a manager who takes credit for their team's hard work just to get a promotion is being selfish in an unhealthy way. It may benefit them in the short term, but it demotivates the team.

In life, you have the freedom to do anything. But every action has a reaction. That reaction may not come right away, but it will eventually come when you least expect it, either as a blessing if you did something right or a lesson if you did something wrong.

So finally, how do you know what's right and wrong?

You look at the intention behind your choices. You need to ask yourself three key questions:

- Is this intention rooted in love or fear?

- Will this help me grow without stepping on someone else?

- Am I willing to take responsibility for how my actions affect those around me?

Right and wrong aren't always black and white. But when your intention is honest, self-aware, and kind, you rarely go wrong. Just like this, you can distinguish between right belief and wrong belief, both internally and externally, through the lens of intention.

If your intention is good—where everyone gains something positive—then your belief is right, even if people around you disagree.

If your intention is bad—where you gain at the expense of others—even if society applauds, that belief is wrong.

You can always measure the quality of your beliefs using a simple filter, knowing that there is right and wrong, good and bad. The difference lies in intention.

If your internal experience is good and your intention is good, then follow it with courage, even if the external world doesn't agree with you. Everything born of good intention is right, regardless of whether anyone else believes it.

If an external belief is good in intention, then embrace it, even if your internal experience feels temporarily good but is actually unhealthy. Because, at the end of the day, everyone—including you—should be safe and happy.

So, your internal beliefs shouldn't remain trapped in fear—fear of society, fear of failure, or fear of standing out. Nor should they remain chained to the blind repetition of external beliefs or unexamined internal beliefs.

Instead, your beliefs must serve the greater good in a higher sense, where you are responsible for your actions, yourself, your family, your society, and the world you share. As humans with unique minds, unique circumstances, and unique perspectives, instead of valuing your uniqueness, most of you abandon it. You follow external beliefs simply because they are loud. Or you cling blindly to internal beliefs, even when they harm you. And in both cases, you lose balance, you lose freedom, and you lose the very essence that makes you human. The real balance is choosing beliefs rooted in healthy intention, aligned with your unique truth, and directed toward the greater good. That is the only way to honor both your individuality and your shared space on earth responsibly.

Taizer

The last bell rang, and children ran out of the school gates. Taizer came out with his friends, scanning the crowd out of habit for Tara. She wasn't there.

He frowned but shrugged it off. Maybe she left early… Anyway, she always walks slowly; maybe Dad picked her up, he thought. And left for home.

When he entered the house, his mother looked up in surprise. "You are early today… Where's Tara?"

Taizer blinked, confused. "I thought she had already reached home."

Silence fell. His mother's smile faded. She quickly called Tara's friends. None of them had seen her after school.

Minutes turned into an hour. The father rushed home; calls were made to teachers, then to the police. The tension grew heavier with each unanswered question.

Taizer sat frozen on the sofa, and fear crawled up his spine. Where is she? Every memory of ignoring her, of mocking her, of shrugging off her care hit him like a storm. Tears stung his eyes. What if something happened? What if... I never see her again?

His father's voice cracked while speaking to the police. His mother paced the floor restlessly, her eyes red with worry. The whole house felt like it was collapsing under grief. And Taizer stood there in the middle of it all, feeling the crushing weight of guilt because he had taken his sister's presence for granted.

Just when the panic reached its height, the front gate opened. There stood the grandmother, holding Tara's hand. Tara was smiling, clutching a small bag. The whole family rushed forward, relief flooding the air.

"Where were you?" Her mother cried, hugging Tara tight.

Before the little girl could speak, the grandmother chuckled softly. "She was planning a little surprise for you," she said. "Since her brother isn't being kind these days, she asked me to help. So after school, I picked her up, and we went shopping together… for Mother's Day."

The room fell silent. Tara pulled out a tiny handmade card and a small gift wrapped in shiny paper. She held it to her mother with wide, innocent eyes. "Happy Mother's Day," she signed and gestured sweetly, her smile brighter than ever. The mother's tears flowed instantly, and she hugged her daughter tight. The father chuckled in relief, shaking his head.

But Taizer… Taizer stood frozen, watching his sister. His throat ached. All the hours of fear, all the guilt of not being kind, crashed against the simple purity of her act.

Grandmother looked at him knowingly, her eyes twinkling. And with a playful wink toward the parents, she added, "Sometimes it takes a little plotting to remind us what matters most." Just like a conspirator, she signaled that her plan had worked.

That night, Taizer lingered in Tara's room long after she had fallen asleep. He watched her breathing, steady and soft, her hands loosely curled over the blanket. The house was quiet now, but inside him, the echoes of those terrifying hours still roared. Hours when Tara was gone, hours when the world had no color.

The door gave a soft, familiar creak as Grandmother stepped inside the room. Her eyes, usually sharp, softened almost imperceptibly as they fell upon the sight: her grandson, Taizer, was hunched by his sister's bedside. His young face was a study in contrasts, a raw mix of guilt and overwhelming tenderness. Without a word, Grandmother moved, her movements slow and deliberate, and settled into the chair next to him.

"You look restless, child," she finally whispered, the sound barely disturbing the quiet of the room.

Taizer swallowed hard, his throat suddenly tight. "I thought I lost her today, Grandma." His voice broke on the final word, a hairline fracture of emotion. "I thought I'd never see her again… And suddenly nothing else mattered. Not school. Not friends. Not grades. Just her."

Grandmother's eyes held a quiet, ancient knowing that seemed to gleam in the dim light. She gently placed a wrinkled hand on his shoulder, a weight of reassurance. "And yet," she murmured, "you've let those very things come between you before."

Taizer's head dropped, his shame a visible burden. "I know. I shouted at her. I pushed her away. I thought…if I kept her at a distance, people would stop laughing at me. At Taksh's jokes." He clenched his fists, the tips of his fingers white. "But the truth is…I was just scared."

Grandmother tilted her head, studying the contours of his confession. "Scared of what, my dear?"

"Of losing my place. Of being seen as weak."

A heavy silence descended between them. Then, Grandmother's voice, softer now, pierced the quiet. "And what do you think made Taksh say those things about your sister?"

Taizer frowned, replaying Taksh's mocking, cruel words in his head. His anger flared momentarily, a brief heat, but then it cooled and softened into something different—something like painful understanding. "He doesn't really hate Tara," Taizer realized, his voice steadier now. "He hates himself for not having scores as excellent as mine. He just wanted to hurt me for getting a higher rank than him. And he used her to do it."

Grandmother offered a faint smile, a complex mixture of sadness for the boy's realization and pride in his insight. "Ah, so you see it now. His intention was jealousy. And what is your Tara's intention? Even when you were shouting in your anger?"

Taizer looked back at his sleeping sister, her face peaceful as if the world had never wounded her. "Her intention…was affection. Always affection. Even when I didn't deserve it."

Grandmother squeezed his shoulder gently. "Yes, then remember this, Taizer. Marks and ranks will fade. But intention…intention shapes who you truly are. Taksh's path is heavy with jealousy. Yours doesn't have to be. And Taras, she's already walking with light."

For the first time in days, Taizer let out a long breath. The storm inside him eased. He took his sister's hand in his own, small and warm.

"I won't let ego blind me again," he whispered.

Grandmother rose quietly, leaving the siblings in that pool of lamplight, her lips curving into the smallest smile. She knew this night would stay with him longer than any lesson taught in school.

The next morning, the sunlight felt different to Taizer—warmer and clearer. He walked to school with Tara, this time slowing his steps so she could match his pace. She glanced up at him, unsure, but when he gently held her hand at the crossing, a joyful smile curved her lips.

At school, Taizer ignored Taksh and his friends. That evening, when they returned home, Grandmother noticed the change; the way Taizer walked beside his sister, his shoulders seemed free. She didn't say a word, only exchanged a knowing glance with their mother. She gave a wink, almost mischievous, as if to say, "It is a truth all siblings eventually discover: they always find their way back, always."

Tara

Tara, though the same age as her brother and his friend Taksh, often seemed older in ways that couldn't be measured by years. She carried a quiet wisdom, a gentleness that neither Taizer nor Taksh fully understood.

What made her so mature at a young age?

It started on an ordinary afternoon. Tara was sitting on the floor, doing her homework, when she suddenly felt something strange—a heaviness in her stomach, a kind of pain she'd never felt before. She shifted in her seat, trying to ignore it, but the discomfort grew. When she went to the bathroom, her breath caught—a faint red stain on her pants.

Her heart raced. For a moment, she didn't know what was happening. She thought she might be hurt. She didn't call for anyone; she just stood there frozen, unsure. Then, quietly, she called out, "Mom?"

Her mother came in, took one look at her pale face, and instantly understood. Without a word, she wrapped Tara in her arms. "It's okay," she whispered. "It's normal. You've just grown up a little."

That evening, her mother sat with her, explaining gently what was happening inside her body—how every month, her body prepared for something it didn't even know it was capable of yet. She taught her how to use a pad, how to track her days, and how to rest when the cramps got too much.

At first, Tara felt embarrassed. The first few days were messy and awkward. She was scared she might stain her uniform, scared her brothers might notice. But her mother was her quiet guardian. She would quietly slip an extra pad into her bag, remind her to drink water, and smile as if to say, You'll get used to it.

And she did.

By the fourth month, Tara started recognizing the signs. It always began the same way: a dull heaviness in her stomach, as if a stone had settled inside. Then came the cramps, sharp and twisting, that made her curl up on her bed, her hands pressed against her belly. Some days, the pain would stay for hours, pulsing like a heartbeat she couldn't control. Her legs would ache too, and her lower back felt like it carried invisible weights. The first few times, she did cry, quietly, into her pillow, not wanting to worry her mother.

The nights were the hardest. Sleep came in patches, interrupted by cramps and a strange, restless feeling she couldn't name. Sometimes, she'd wake up drenched in sweat, her mood swinging between irritation and tears for no reason at all. There were moments she hated her body—the stains, the pain, the sudden exhaustion. She felt different from her younger self.

The world went on as usual, while inside her, everything was changing.

Her mother noticed, of course. Some evenings, she would find Tara sitting quietly by the window, her expression unreadable. Without saying much, her mother would hand her a cup of warm chocolate milk and say softly, "It's okay to rest. You don't have to be strong every day."

Over the next few months, Tara's emotions began to follow patterns. A few days before her cycle, she'd feel everything more deeply. A small word from a friend could bring her to tears. A random memory could make her chest ache for no reason.

Her periods were teaching Tara to understand what her mother had gone through every month without complaint. When the cramps hit, she learned to breathe through them, to slow down, and to take care of herself.

It wasn't easy—there were moments she felt frustrated, irritated for no reason, or just tired of it all. But slowly, she learned to live with it. She continued to attend school, interact with friends, and enjoy laughter despite the pain in her body. And when the period was done, she'd go about as if nothing had changed. That cycle of pain and calm, of losing and regaining balance, became her quiet teacher. It showed her how to be patient, how to be kind to herself, and how to understand the other women and men in her life.

And that teacher, though she didn't realize it then, was what made Tara grow into the most grounded and most empathic one among the three of them.

Woman

Every woman goes through it in her own way, but the essence remains the same: pain arrives, demands her attention, and reshapes the way she relates to herself and the world around her.

Alright, readers, before proceeding, a small note to men:

Periods are painful and emotional for every woman, no matter how frustrated people get listening to her talk about them.

I get it; it's her own job to get used to it, but honestly, she is trying her best. Trust me. We all are.

Do you know what happens in the process of handling moods during her period? Life gets in her way... as a daughter, as a sister, as a student, as a career person, as a wife, as a homemaker, as a mother, and as a physically impressive being.

So, along with the pain and emotional hormonal changes her body is throwing at her, she is also handling life.

And you know what? Getting her period is actually a relief for her, too. The week before is really awful. When a woman finally starts her period, she feels like she has more clarity and her intuition is better, but the PMS week is a fog, which is inbuilt.

So guys, please excuse her the next time you hear about it and feel frustrated.

Now coming to the point,

To my fellow women out there,

I know period pain made you so strong that it made you handle any kind of pain life throws at you. Those mixed emotions literally make you cry each and every month for no reason or maybe for every reason. Those feelings associated with your period can make you question your entire self-worth. Those periods you have every month remind you of all your struggles. Even if you achieved what you wanted, or even if you are someone who has so much self-love and is super confident, you still cry during those periods.

Period moods are inbuilt for us women. Sometimes there is no reason for it. But we add extra reasons and make it more emotional by blaming life or the people around us. So all I want to say is: you are doing great, life is life-ing, and don't make periods more complex by adding extra reasons.

If you still feel like adding an extra reason, here's this observation. We all know that periods are directly associated with childbirth, right? So maybe, just maybe, these cycles are our body's way of preparing us for that—emotionally, physically, all of it. Those cramps, those tears? They're building our strength, teaching us about our bodies, and maybe even getting us ready for the marathon of labor one day.

So keep tracking your cycle, and keep learning your

body. Tell yourself, “This is my period mood.” It helps, even if you still cry. Actually, to be honest, crying helps us release our tension and feel better. Afterwards, we naturally indulge in a piece of cake, of course. Yes, self-care is important—not just by eating cake, though. I get it.

But there is one thing we always regret after a period, and that is showing frustration toward the people around us. That's something that is difficult to fix, I agree. But keep working on it.

And this period especially reminds us of our people. Those who get it, who don't need us to explain, who just show up with a hug or simply with their presence. To the partner, friends, and family—especially the great men out there—thank you. You see us at our rawest and love us anyway. Your understanding is a gift, and it makes the journey lighter.

So, to every woman dealing with this period rollercoaster: you are amazing.

Pain, in the form of periods, became a universal teacher to women. While crying the pain out, it whispers, "If it hurts this much for you, imagine how it hurts for someone else." That reflection is the seed of understanding. Women, because of repeated cycles of pain, often develop an instinct to notice and nurture pain in others.

Many women go through their cycles silently, still studying, working, caring, and creating, even when their bodies ache. This silent endurance builds an inner strength that is rarely spoken of. It's why, even at young ages, girls like Tara can appear more grounded, more understanding, and more mature than boys around them.

Women, by nature of period cycles, encounter pain earlier and more regularly. She is almost trained by life itself to hold both her own sufferings as well as others.

It's not that women are born more mature; it's that pain visits them earlier and more often, and pain, when embraced, is the fastest path to understanding compassion.

Taksh

That lack of pain makes a human less empathic, more self-centered, and more egoistic, leading to bad intentions.

Women, in many ways, are ahead in this regard. Pain visits them earlier and more regularly through their cycles. It makes them more empathic, more understanding, and more compassionate. And when life's other struggles arrive, they do not break as easily. Pain has already carved resilience into them.

But how do others understand the value of compassion, which is a key to learning the difference between Right and Wrong?

By experiencing pain themselves, especially the kind of pain they once caused others. This is the simple, eternal principle of cause and effect. Every action carries its reaction. Not as a punishment, but as a teaching.

Let's consider Taksh. He was so pampered from childhood, being a single child for his parents, shielded from pain, and never truly tested. Because he never experienced deep pain, he couldn't understand the loving intention behind his parents' strictness about studies. To him, discipline felt like control, not love. This lack of empathy became a breeding ground for frustration, which he spread by bullying Taizer and Tara with a contagious ego.

Then, one day, Taksh proposed to his crush. Her rejection was blunt: "You are not the first ranker like Taizer."

Pause. That was a moment of true pain.

For the first time, Taksh questioned the belief system he had inherited. Was love really something to be measured by grades, by ranks, by comparison? Was that fair? Was that right?

As he wrestled with the sting of that rejection, the answer appeared, not in books or from teachers, but in the two people he had hurt the most—Taizer and Tara.

One person had shining grades and relentless drive, while the other faced quiet struggles and took slower steps. By all the standards Taksh had been taught to live by, their bond should have cracked. Grades should have divided them. Success should have set them apart.

Yet, despite the cracks Taksh himself had tried to carve between them, their bonding had survived. It blossomed in Tara's soft patience, in Taksh's awakening regret, and in the way they always seemed to find their way back to each other.

That is a true sibling bond. It is not measured by numbers but strengthened by intention. It is not limited by what the world defines as "success," but expanded by values.

And for the first time in his life, Taksh understood a profound truth: the value of love, the value of people, could never be measured by numbers.

It could only be measured by the heart.

The next afternoon, when school ended, Taizer and Tara were walking home together. Tara, as always, rushed to catch her brother at the gate, her small hand clutching his sleeve.

Now, just as they were about to leave, our conflicted young man, Taksh, appeared. He was standing awkwardly by the roadside. His usual swagger was completely gone; he looked nervous, almost shy.

"Taizer…" he began, his voice low.

Taizer stopped, his brows furrowed. "What is it now, Taksh?"

Taksh hesitated, his eyes flicking toward Tara. For a moment, guilt clouded his face. Then, with a shaky breath, he spoke.

"I'm sorry."

Words hung in the air, raw and heavy.

"I shouldn't have made fun of Tara. Or you. I thought… I truly thought grades were everything. That's what I was taught, you see. And when I couldn't match you, I got angry. Jealous," his voice cracked. "But then… I realized I was wrong. True affection isn't measured by grades. I saw it…in you two. You... you never gave up on each other."

Taizer blinked, caught off guard. His anger, sharp and ready, softened at the sight of Taksh's trembling honesty. Tara tilted her head, watching silently, her eyes filled with the quiet understanding that had always been her gift.

Taizer finally exhaled, his own walls breaking down. "It hurt, Taksh. What you did…it hurt. But if you mean this apology, then we can start over."

Taksh nodded quickly, relief washing over him. "I do, I really do."

And in that small, unpolished moment, on a dusty school road, with nothing grand but three children finding their way, friendship was reborn. It wasn't perfect, not without scars, but it became stronger than before.

Pain

That's the role of pain in life.

Pain, emotional or physical, is unbearable. It's bitter, sharp, and often feels unfair. But just like a medicine, its bitterness hides a quiet healing.

Think of it like learning to ride a bicycle. You know the feeling. You fall, the skin on your knee breaks, it bleeds, and it burns. The wound stings not just because it hurts, but because it reminds you that you failed to balance. You limp for a few days. But then, one day, you do. You push past the fear, hold the handles tighter, and pedal again—and this time, you don't fall.

All that happened there was growth, pure self-growth. It tells you, if you feel this much pain, how much pain is caused if you don't ride a bicycle carefully. And that, is compassion taught via pain.

Pain was part of the process. It was never punishment; it was preparation.

Yes, not everyone learns the same way. Some people master the bicycle without a single fall. Others fall again and again until they finally get it right. But in the end, both reach the same road. Both are capable. Both can go as far as they wish. The difference is only in resilience, in how long one can endure the pain before finding their rhythm.

And yes, pain actually hurts. It drains you, and it makes

you question, "Why me?" But when you sit with it long enough, something happens. Out of the tears, out of the ache, a quiet strength begins to form.

It arrives not as punishment, but as direction—a silent compass from the universe, guiding you back when you lose your way. It often comes when your ego grows louder than your compassion, when you can't differentiate what is right and what is wrong. It shows up exactly when you need to see what your eyes refused to see before.

Just like a woman and her cycles. Pain, in the end, is not the end. It's the beginning of knowing yourself. Pain has different forms, just as your circumstances and perspectives are different.

For Taizer, Tara, and Taksh, pain came wearing different faces—fear, failure, separation, guilt—but each form carried the same message: to learn compassion and to be able to differentiate between right and wrong.

No teacher, parent, or book can reach as deeply as pain does, because pain speaks the language of the soul. It dissolves wrong beliefs, the fear of not fitting in, the need to prove, and the blindness of the ego. It teaches you that there is good and bad, right and wrong, not in the world's opinions but in the intention behind what you do. If your intention is pure, your path, no matter how uncertain, will eventually lead you to light. If the intention is unhealthy, selfish, or fearful, even the brightest road will turn dark.

Pain educates and redirects. Every challenge, every

heartbreak, every failure is simply a classroom—a place where the soul learns compassion, patience, and purpose.

And when you finally understand that, pain loses its sting. It becomes what it was always meant to be. A teacher who arrives when the lesson of love must be learned again.

Taizer, who had always been driven to achieve top grades, now approached his studies with a calm focus. Fear no longer dictated his every move; instead, he learned to balance ambition with understanding, letting his love for learning guide him.

Tara, too, began to blossom in her own way. She approached studies with curiosity and patience, supported by the same love and freedom that had nurtured her creativity in exploring herself.

Taksh, who had once been quick to judge and mirror the ego-driven behaviors around him, began to see the real cost of bullying. He understood that cruelty often stems from fear, envy, or misunderstanding, and that recognizing this truth could guide him toward compassion rather than resentment.

Together, the trio grew not just in skill or knowledge, but in wisdom. They understood that the world may challenge them, that others may project fear or envy, but their choices—guided by love and clarity—shape who they truly become. Pain from the world, from friends, or even from loved ones, becomes manageable when filtered through awareness—when one can distinguish healthy intention from unhealthy intention, guidance from ego, and love from fear.

Pain teaches you what books or people cannot. It teaches you to distinguish internal beliefs—the truth you feel in your heart via self-sense experience—from external beliefs—the rules, judgments, and expectations imposed by society, friends, or family. Both can be right, both can be wrong, but their impact depends on intention. A belief guided by healthy intention inspires growth; one guided by unhealthy selfishness sows hurt.

Empathy and Compassion: Not the same thing

Empathy and compassion are often used interchangeably, but they are not the same. While they are closely related, they operate in fundamentally different ways and lead to very different outcomes in how you relate to others—and yourself.

Empathy is the ability to feel and understand another person's pain. It is emotional resonance. When someone is hurting, empathy allows you to step into their experience, to sense what they are feeling, and to acknowledge the weight of that pain. Empathy is powerful, but it is also momentary. You feel for someone, and then you move on from that situation. The feeling may linger, but empathy itself does not require action, change, or growth. It is awareness without obligation.

Compassion, on the other hand, begins where empathy ends. Compassion is what remains after you step away from the situation. It is what you carry forward. Compassion is learning—learning from another person's pain or from your own. It is the internal shift that reshapes how you see the world, how you treat others, and how you respond when similar pain appears again.

A simple way to understand the difference is empathy says, "I feel your pain." Compassion says, "I will let this pain change how I live."

Imagine witnessing someone go through a profound loss. Empathy allows you to grieve with them, to feel the heaviness of their sorrow, and to sit with them in that moment. But when you leave, empathy alone fades with distance and time. Compassion, however, stays. It may show up later as patience with others who are grieving, deeper kindness toward strangers, or a renewed commitment to be present for the people you love. The pain becomes a teacher.

This distinction matters because empathy without compassion can become emotionally exhausting. Feeling deeply without integrating meaning or growth can leave you drained, overwhelmed, or numb. Compassion transforms emotional exposure into wisdom. It turns pain into understanding and understanding into intention.

Compassion does not require staying in harmful situations or carrying suffering forever. In fact, it often requires moving away. But unlike empathy, compassion ensures the experience is not wasted. Something is learned. Something is softened. Something changes. It is the quiet evolution that happens after pain has passed, shaping who you become long after the moment itself is over.

Parents

Taksh, utterly drained after a long day, dropped his bag, went straight to his mother, and laid his head in her lap. Her hands gently stroked his hair, and without realizing it, Taksh drifted into sleep.

Hours passed. Evening turned into night. His father came home and saw him asleep on the sofa, still curled in his mother's lap. Normally, this was his study time—no excuses. But something about Taksh's face made his father stop. The boy looked worn out, drained of every ounce of energy. For once, his father didn't wake him. He just stood there for a moment, sighed, and walked away.

Taksh woke up much later, in the middle of the night. His head felt heavy, his heart restless. He turned, trying to fall back asleep, but his eyes caught something that made him pause.

His father was lying next to him. The man who was always strict about studies, who demanded discipline and never seemed to bend, was now asleep by his side. For a moment, Taksh just stared. Something stirred deep inside him, something he couldn't name. He slid back under the blanket, feeling strangely lighter, and slept.

The next morning, as sunlight streamed in, Taksh found his mother in the kitchen. Still rubbing sleep from his eyes, he asked, "Mom, why did Dad sleep next to me last night?"

His mother glanced at him and said, "Because you

looked so tired, so drained. He was worried about you. He thought maybe, if he stayed close, you'd rest better."

Taksh froze. For a moment, the words sank as his chest tightened. All this time, he had thought his father's strictness was harsh. But now he saw it: behind the rules, behind the raised voice, there was worry. There was love.

"Mom," he whispered after a long silence, "can I ask you something?"

His mother looked up from chopping vegetables, her eyes soft. "Of course."

"If Dad loves me so much," Taksh said slowly, "why is he so strict with me about studies? Even when I'm doing much better than most of my classmates?"

His mother put down the knife, wiped her hands on her apron, and placed a gentle touch on his shoulders. Her voice was gentle but steady. "Do you remember, Taksh? A few years ago, when you cried so much because you missed a rank in school just because of one mark?"

Taksh frowned, thinking. Then it came back to him: the day he lost his place on the toppers list, not because he wasn't capable, but because he had spent his time procrastinating, lost in distractions and cartoons. He had cried bitterly, blaming himself, feeling worthless.

"Yes…" he admitted quietly.

His mother nodded. "Your father saw the pain in your

eyes. He saw how much you wanted to do well but how easily distraction pulled you away. From that day, he decided he would never let you fall into that trap again. His strictness…it isn't anger. It's his way of protecting you from the pain of your own procrastination and from distractions."

Taksh sat still, her words sinking into him like warm rain. He quietly replayed his mother's words. His father's face from last night came back to him, not stern, not scolding, but resting beside him out of worry.

His mother sat next to him, her voice becoming softer, almost like she was speaking to herself as much as him.

"You see, Taksh… parents are the most misunderstood people in a child's life. You see only our faces today—strict, worried, sometimes even angry. But you don't see the storm we carry inside. We don't get a manual on how to raise a child. We stumble, we learn, we fall, and we rise, all while trying to make sure you don't fall the same way we did."

She paused, as if searching for the right words. "A father's strictness isn't because he doesn't love you; it is because he loves you so much he fears losing you to your own distractions. A mother's scolding isn't because she doubts you; it's because she has seen the world and wants to toughen you so it doesn't break you."

Taksh listened, his chest tightening with every word.

"Do you know what's hardest for a parent?" she

continued. "It's that we are judged only by our actions, not our intentions. When we give freedom, people say we are careless. When we set boundaries, people say we are controlling. When we push you to study, you think we are harsh. When we let you relax, you think we don't care about your future. Whatever we do, it feels wrong to someone. But in truth, all of it—every word, every rule, every sleepless night—is born from love. A love so deep that it sometimes looks like the opposite."

She took a deep breath. "We don't always say it right. We don't always do it right. But Taksh, if you look past the surface, you will see no one will ever love you with a purer intention than your parents."

Something inside Taksh cracked open then. He thought of his father lying beside him, of the countless evenings his mother stayed up late while he studied, and of the sacrifices he never noticed. They weren't enemies. They were bridges, flawed and imperfect, but carrying him forward with every step.

For the first time, Taksh didn't just see his parents. He understood them.

Parents, too, are shaped by the same dance of internal and external beliefs.

Internally, a parent's belief is born from their own experiences. Perhaps they were only praised for being "strong" and taught that vulnerability was unsafe. Their tears were met with discomfort, anger, or shame. Now,

when their child cries, something tightens in their chest. They rush to fix, distract, or shut it down.
These lived experiences become their internal compass—"I don't want my child to suffer as I did."

Externally, they are taught what "good parenting" looks like by relatives, neighbors, schools, and society. A good parent is told to raise a successful child, a child who gets high grades, lands a secure job, and follows the accepted milestones of life. These external beliefs are loud, constant, and full of pressure.
Caught between the two, fear takes root.
- Fear of repeating their own childhood struggles.
- Fear of being judged by society if their child doesn't fit the mold
- Fear that if they let go of control, they will fail their duty as parents.

Fear makes parents do strange things. It makes them raise their voices when actually they are just worried. It makes them set rules when they are really just trying to protect the child. It looks like control, but for parents, it feels like the only way to keep the child safe. And that love sometimes gets hidden behind strictness. The parents' true intention—love, protection, care—is wrapped in the armor of fear. The child only sees the armor, not the heart beneath it.

But just as children must balance their internal and external beliefs, so must parents. When they learn to trust their love more than fear, the armor softens. They see that their child's freedom is not a threat but a gift.

Parents are not all-knowing. They, too, are students of life, unlearning outdated external beliefs and healing from harmful internal experiences, while learning new truths through the very children they raise.

Parents are human too. They love so deeply and fear just as deeply. And sometimes that fear hides the love.
Maybe growing up isn't about choosing between fear and love. Maybe it's about learning to let love guide you, even when fear is loud.

Fear

Fear hides in the quiet corners of every heart. For Taizer, it was the fear of losing his friends if he stood by his sister. For Taksh, it was the fear of not being enough in his parents' eyes. For their parents, it was the fear of a future where their children might struggle if they didn't push them hard enough.

And when fear becomes too heavy, the ego is born. Taizer's silence toward his sister, Taksh's bullying, and even the raised voices of parents were all defenses, shields built to protect their own hearts that were only afraid of breaking.

Yet, when the layers were peeled back, the truth was clear. Behind the Takshs' father's strictness was worry. Behind Taizer's frustration were confused beliefs.

The balance, then, is not to kill fear or silence the ego, but to understand them. To ask: What is the intention behind this action? Is it born of love or fear/ego? Because intentions let us know what is right and what is wrong, what is healthy and what is unhealthy. What is good, and what is bad.
And once fear is understood, once ego is seen for what it truly is, the armor falls away. What remains is love—simple, unshaken, unafraid.

And so, Taizer, Tara, and Taksh learned what the universe had been teaching all along: that pain is a guide, and ego is a defense born out of fear. But love is the truth that always finds its way back via pain and understanding the intentions behind every action.

New Life needs Diplomacy

At eighteen, the world expected Taizer, Tara, and Taksh to take the usual road: college admissions, career planning, lectures, and exams. Every elder they met asked the same question: "Engineering? Medicine?" The three nodded politely, but inside, they already carried a different answer.

For the last six years, whenever they came together, their conversations had circled back to one topic: food. Not fancy cafe food, but the laughter-filled snacks they made in Tara's kitchen. While other kids hung out in malls or movie theaters, their favorite hangout spot was the warm, cluttered family kitchen.

Tara, exploring herself, found her heart in the kitchen. Because both parents were working, and also out of curiosity, she started experimenting with recipes. Her dishes were never ordinary. A touch of spice here, a playful garnish there, her food carried the flavor of love, and the boys? They were her willing guinea pigs, cheering her with every bite.

One evening, after a long day at school, the trio sat sprawled on the sofa, hungry and too tired to cook. They scrolled through Uber Eats, debating what to order, when they stumbled across a phrase they hadn't seen before: "Cloud kitchen."

Curious, they tapped. They read. And slowly, the idea began to simmer in their minds. A restaurant without a restaurant. A place that existed in the heart of a kitchen, reaching people through food alone.

"This," Taksh whispered, his eyes wide, "this is us."

That night, they researched everything about cloud kitchens, delivery apps, and how they work. Their school projects had never made them so alive. And somewhere deep down, they all knew: they had found their first dream.

With pocket money saved from birthdays and festivals, they bought ingredients. Tara led the experiments, while Taizer invested in learning marketing and sales by sharing some recipes on YouTube, and Taksh studied finance strategies. What started as a playful idea began to take shape: their own cloud kitchen. Every time Tara created something new, they invited friends and neighbors to try it. With notebooks in hand, the boys collected reviews, scribbled down suggestions, and debated improvements. Each feedback loop made Tara sharper, more inventive, and more confident.

And beyond the pots and pans, they studied. Their evenings were a blend of flavors and spreadsheets, thanks to the endless library of the internet, which provided case studies of cloud kitchens, articles, and business models.

Friends and family, though supportive, didn't see the seriousness burning in their eyes. To the outside world, it looked like fun. For all three, it was passion.

When the three finally revealed their dream, to start a

cloud kitchen right after school, the room fell silent. Their parents looked at each other, then at them, and almost in unison said no.

"No one skips higher studies for cooking experiments." Taizer's father insisted.

"Finish your degree first, then think about businesses," Taksh's mother added firmly.

Every relative and every neighbor echoed the same advice: bachelor's first, everything else later.

The words fell heavy on the three. Their united dream felt fragile. That night, they stayed together, disappointment hanging thick in the air.

It was Taksh who finally spoke. "Do you remember when I tied my self-worth to grades? My parents weren't being bad… They were just fearful. They thought without grades, I'd fail in life."

He turned to Taizer. "And you… Do you remember how fear blinded you, too? You couldn't see Tara's good intentions because you were scared of losing face with your friends."

Both Taizer and Tara went quiet. Taksh's words cut through.

"So maybe," Taksh continued, "our parents aren't against us. Maybe they're just afraid—afraid of us failing, afraid of society laughing, afraid of not giving us security. Fear is

loud. But love is behind it."

The three exchanged a look. They weren't disappointed anymore. They understood the situation.

And that's when an idea sparked: what if we showed them that this isn't just a dream? What if we showed them our six years of background work, our research, and our small but steady experiments?

Taizer leaned forward. "We have the perfect opportunity at the upcoming graduate ceremony event. "Everyone will be there. If we cook and manage it like a real kitchen, they'll see with their own eyes. Not just our passion. But our capability."

Tara's eyes lit up. Taksh grinned. The disappointment melted into determination.

The plan was simple but daring: to eliminate fear of parents with proof, to replace doubt with action.

At the after-grad ceremony tea party, held in their own backyard, they set out a table that didn't look like any other. Tara had filled it with trays of golden muffins, crisp croissants, and eclairs drizzled with chocolate. Alongside them, she brewed coffee laced with cinnamon, a warm, spiced aroma that floated through the air and pulled everyone in.

Neighbors, relatives, and family friends came closer. One bite, and their expressions changed. Surprise turned into delight.

“Where did you buy these?”

“We didn't buy them,” Taksh proudly said. “We made them. All of us.”

Compliments poured in. Everyone asked for recipes and was so impressed. For a brief moment, the three friends stood taller than ever. This was their passion speaking for itself.

When the crowd left, the house grew quieter. Their parents sat them down.

“You did very well today,” Taizer’s father began. “Everyone loved it.”

A smile flickered across Tara's face, but it faded when he added, “But this…this cannot be your future. Cloud kitchens? Bakeries? No. You need a degree, a stable path. This is just a hobby.”

The words hit harder than they expected. For a moment, none of them spoke. Taizer clenched his fists under the table. Tara looked at her muffins, as if they had suddenly lost their glow.

Taksh’s shoulders sank, but his mind didn't collapse with them. For the first time, he saw clearly: fear cannot be eliminated by others. His parents' beliefs and their insistence on degrees and safety weren't born overnight, and they couldn't be erased overnight either. Fear was sticky; it clung to people.

Taksh looked at Tara and Taizer. "We can't fight this," he said softly. "Not with anger. Not with force. Fear only grows stronger when you attack it."

"Then what do we do?" Tara whispered, her voice trembling.

"Diplomacy," Taksh replied.

Diplomacy does not mean being fake; it means choosing the right words to avoid unnecessary drama and to bridge gaps instead of widening them.

After countless failed attempts to convince his parents, Taksh had run out of options. He had argued, reasoned, and even pleaded, but nothing broke through the wall of fear his father carried. Finally, one evening, he sat down with his father and laid out his last solution.

"Give me one year," Taksh said firmly. If I succeed, I'll continue with this cloud kitchen. Otherwise, I'll follow your path.

It wasn't a rebellion. It wasn't disrespectful. It was diplomacy. His father, weary but unable to find a counter, reluctantly agreed. Not with pride, not with joy, but with disinterested silences. A silence that lingered in the house like an unspoken storm.

For the next whole year, Taksh lived under that silence. Every sale, every review carried a double weight—not just proving himself to the world, but breaking through the quiet wall his father had built.

Yet strangely, the silence did not destroy him. Taksh knew something now; his father's harshness and his father's silence were not born of hate. They were born of fear. Fear, out of love. That knowledge shielded him and turned the silence into pressure, yes, but also into fuel.

And slowly, he tried to chip away at the silence with diplomacy. Not fake words, but smart ones. He exaggerated his progress, shared glowing customer reviews, and presented sales reports like medals. He highlighted every little success, not to boast, but to ease his father's fear.

We are living in a world where there is a constant mismatch between beliefs—between generations, between friends, and even within families. Everyone carries their own version of truth, built from personal experiences, fears, and circumstances since birth. In such a world, the greatest survival skill isn't aggression or rebellion—it's diplomacy.

Because let me be honest, trying to change another person's belief is almost impossible. Beliefs are not built overnight, and they cannot be dismantled overnight. They are shaped by years of conditioning, by the stories people tell themselves to feel safe. Expecting to change someone's entire inner system with a single conversation is like expecting the sea to calm down because you whispered at it.

That's where diplomacy comes in.

Diplomacy isn't about being fake; it's about being wise. It's the ability to choose your words carefully, to say what matters without setting fire to the bridge you are standing on. It's about knowing when to speak, when to listen, and when to let silence speak to you. True diplomacy is not manipulation—it's emotional intelligence.

When every human walks with a unique combination of beliefs, fears, perspectives, and circumstances, conflict becomes inevitable. But diplomacy is what helps you keep love alive in the room, even when understanding is missing. It allows space for two truths to exist without one overpowering the other.

Diplomacy is what lets a child talk to a fearful parent without disrespecting them. It's what lets a friend disagree without turning into an enemy. It's what makes relationships—whether personal, professional, or societal—sustainable in the long run. Because at its heart, diplomacy is not about who wins the argument; it's about who keeps the connection alive.

In a world full of mismatched beliefs, diplomacy becomes the language of peace. It's the art of being honest without being harsh, assertive without being arrogant, and true without being cruel. It reminds you that you don't always need to fight to prove you are right—sometimes choosing the right words at the right time is the highest form of strength.

Emotional Tiredness

Just before completing the one-year deal with their parents, the dream was at its brightest. Sales were strong, reviews glowing, and their little kitchen had become a favorite in the neighborhood. The teenagers felt they had finally proved themselves.

On the very last day of the deal between the teenagers and their parents, a notice landed at their door. A lawsuit. Someone had filed a complaint against their kitchen, claiming that one of their dishes had caused food poisoning at a private event.

The air in the room froze. Tara's hands trembled as she held the paper. Taizer stared blankly at the words, his mind refusing to process. Taksh clenched his jaw at the timing, as if the universe had chosen to test them at their highest peak.

The parents, who had stayed skeptical all year, looked at the trio, eyes heavy with both fear and silently expressing, "We told you so," and seized the moment. "This is enough," Taizer's father said firmly. "We gave you a year, and now see where it's brought you. This is why we asked you to get a proper degree.'

At home, the tension was worse than the lawsuit itself. Every word from the parents carried fear; every silence felt like disapproval. For them, this was proof, not of their kids' courage, but of the risks they had always feared.

The three were exhausted. Tired of fighting parents, tired of fighting fear, tired of proving themselves to everyone. And yet, deep inside, the dream was still alive, flickering.

The lawsuit wasn't just a legal challenge. It was a mirror, forcing them to look at themselves and ask:
Do we give up, or do we go on?

That night, none of them had an answer.
Taksh, who had carried the banner of diplomacy, was so exhausted. He is already facing silent treatment from his father. But now, fighting both the law outside and the fear inside his own home, it was too much.

He sat alone one night, papers scattered before him, his chest tight. His friends were asleep, his parents' words still echoing in his head. For the first time, the thought crossed his mind: maybe they are right. Maybe I should give up.

The lawsuit was not just against their kitchen. It felt like a lawsuit against his very dream, his worth, and his belief in himself.

He closed his eyes. Tears pressed at the corners. "How much longer," he whispered, "do I have to keep proving myself?"

The lawsuit was draining every drop of energy from them. Papers, notices, and confusing words from lawyers all felt like a foreign language. Days passed with tension in the air, and nights turned sleepless. Their parents watched silently, waiting for the moment their children would finally give up and admit to their path.

Just when they were almost ready to give up, a man appeared—a well-dressed man, kind, confident, and full of promises.
"I've been hearing about it a lot lately," he said warmly, looking around at their modest setup. "Teenagers running a cloud kitchen that neighbors can't stop talking about? Do you know how rare that is?

Tara blinked. No one outside their little circle had ever spoken to them like that.

He continued, "I tried your eclairs at your graduation tea party—cinnamon, a hint of spice, the texture, the creativity…unbelievable. Frankly, better than what I've had at five-star bakeries. And you're only eighteen! Do you realize the future you could have if someone like me helped carry this forward?"

He leaned closer. "Look, I know about the lawsuit. It's not a big deal. My legal team can sweep it away in days. No stress, no fear. All you have to do is let me come in as a partner. You keep doing what you love—cooking and spreading joy—and I'll handle the boring part—money, law, and management. Together, we'll make this brand famous across the city, maybe even the country."

And indeed, he did sound like he believed in them more than anyone ever had. His praise was genuine; his promises and his confidence are magnetic.

That night, the three sat in their room, silent. The offer glittered like gold.

"Why does it feel…wrong when he said everything right?" Tara whispered.

"Did you feel it too? He's actually solving our problem… but why does it feel like we'll lose something?" said Taizer

"He believes in us," Taksh admitted. "Maybe more than our own parents," but it still feels…empty. Said Taksh

They all paused. Something about his words rang hollow, not because they weren't true—they were painfully accurate—but because he hadn't touched their hearts.

Yes, he had noticed Tara's gift, Taizer's discipline, and Taksh's fire. Yes, he had spoken to their strengths and soothed their wounds. He had touched every corner of their doubt and every crack in their pride.

But not once did he see the evenings in their tiny kitchen when laughter bubbled louder than the pots on the stove. Not once did he know why food mattered to them or why they had chosen this path at all.
And in that silence, they realized the way to touch their heart was never through praise, never through fame, or even proving their parents wrong.

The way to touch their heart was through intention. The intention of creating something together, something born of love, something that fed more than the stomach and the joy it brought.

The man's intention had spoken to their fears and their strengths. It was to shape them into something that fit his vision, not theirs. That's why, even after all his perfect words, their hearts stayed still. Because hearts only move when intentions match.

By morning, the decision was clear. They thanked him, sincerely, because his words had indeed lifted them.
It wasn't easy. But as the door closed, the three of them felt something ignite within.
They realized something profound:
- If this dream were only rebellion, they would've given up by now.
- If it were only a hobby, the lawsuit would've been enough to scare them away.

- But if it was their calling, they would find the strength to continue from nowhere, not in anger, not in stubbornness, but in clarity.

And in that moment, clarity dawned. Because they had finally faced the hardest test of all: the kind that dresses as love, praise, and security. And by refusing, they knew their dream wasn't built on fear or validation—it was built on truth.

Hobby vs True Calling

There is often a very thin line between a hobby and a true calling. Sometimes you push too hard on something that's meant to stay as a hobby, thinking it's your life's work. At times, you may abandon a genuine calling prematurely due to lack of results. Knowing when to stop and when to keep going isn't easy—but there are subtle ways to find out.

It's important to remember that doing the same thing over and over without seeing any real change can be risky. Whether it's at work, in a creative pursuit, or in personal goals, there are times you keep grinding away, hoping persistence alone will make things better. But sometimes, it's wiser to step back and consider whether what you are doing truly fits your skills and interests.

Match quality is the degree to which something suits who you are. Finding the right match often matters more than simple perseverance. After all, if you are doing something that truly fits you, sticking with it becomes natural. You don't have to force motivation; it grows from within.

However, once you have found a good match, there's also a danger in quitting too soon or constantly changing direction. Many of us give up just before things start to turn around. This is surprisingly common and is called commission bias—an urge to do something rather than stay the course. When progress feels slow, you become impatient. You start to believe that taking new action or any action will fix things.

But often, the best thing you can do is do nothing. You can keep going, make small adjustments, and let things unfold in their own time. Growth rarely happens all at once. It takes patience, consistency, and trust in the process.

We live in a world that celebrates action. We are taught to always move forward, to never stand still. Yet sometimes, wisdom lies in stillness. Instead of always thinking, “Don’t just stand there, do something,” it's good you might consider the opposite: "Don’t just do something, stand there.”

It's in those quiet moments—when you pause instead of panic—that clarity often comes. And with clarity, you begin to see whether you are nurturing a hobby or answering a calling.

That strength to move forward even in moments of emotional exhaustion, that quiet persistence when everything feels heavy, is often the truest sign that what you are pursuing is not just a hobby but a calling. Hobbies excite you for a while, but calling pulls you, even when you are too tired to move.

Every challenge, every delay, every obstacle is a molding process. Just as clay meets the potter's hand, your soul meets your purpose through friction, through shaping, and through time. These breaks and tests are not barriers; they are whispers from the universe, saying, “You are not quite ready yet, but you are getting there.”

Just as love involves learning another person's language, their silences, their needs, and their rhythm, your career, passion, and purpose also have their own unique love language. It speaks in lessons and in patience. Learning this love language takes time.

When things don't work out immediately, it doesn't mean the dream has abandoned you. It simply means you and your dream are still learning to understand each other.

The dream is saying, "Wait—you are not yet aligned to me. Let's progress together and reach a mutual understanding."

And one day, when that alignment finally happens—when your effort, emotion, and purpose move in sync—you realize that all the delays, the tears, and the confusion were never obstacles. They were the language of your calling, teaching you how to love your dream the right way—with patience, depth, and unwavering faith.

Let me give you some major signs to say, "Yes, it's my true calling." And please note that these signs can be applied to any part of your life, mainly relationships and career.

1. When it's your true calling, it feels natural. Not necessarily easy, but it somehow manages to nourish your soul instead of draining it. You are putting in effort, sure, but it's the kind of effort that energizes you, not exhausts you. Deep down, you know—this is what you are meant to be doing.

Think about it. When you are faking it or forcing yourself to fit into a role—whether it's a job or a relationship—it's like swimming against the current. You are always tired, even if you did nothing; you are frustrated for unknown reasons, and you have to keep convincing yourself to stick with it. But when you are doing what is meant for you, you don't need to convince yourself. You just keep going because it feels right.

And the challenges don't stop you on this path. They excite you. Here you are not comparing yourself to others, thinking, "Ugh, why are they ahead?" Instead, you are like, "Good for them, but I am on my own path, and I am content with that."

2. Now let's talk about a huge sign, the second one: here you are very eager to learn and update your skills, diving into new ideas, without being pushed. When your career or relationship aligns with your heart, you are naturally driven to improve. You are reading, researching, and practicing—whatever it takes—because you want to, not because you have to.

Let me give you an example. Imagine someone who's always been fascinated by tech. Even in a busy schedule, they're taking online courses, reading about new frameworks, or debugging the code. It's effortless for them. But if that same person is stuck in a job as, say, a builder, if it's just not their thing, they procrastinate. They avoid learning or updating their skills in the construction industry because it feels like a slog. That's a clear sign it's not aligned with their heart. They're just surviving for the paycheck.

3. Coming to the third sign, here you need to look back at your childhood. What are you good at? Maybe you are always reading about chess, building model airplanes, or debating politics with your cousins. As kids, you naturally gravitate toward what lights you up. But then school, exams, and "routine" career advice might have pulled you away.

But those childhood interests often stick with you, even if you don't realize it. Let's say, for example, even if you haven't played chess in years, you still find yourself reading articles about grandmasters or watching matches online. That's what your heart tells you, saying, "Hey, remember this? This is you." So, pay attention to what you are still drawn to, even unknowingly. It's a clue to your true path.

4. And the fourth sign is your personality. From childhood to now, your strengths and behaviors are like a roadmap

to your true calling. Are you patient and focused? Maybe chess or strategy-heavy careers are your thing. Great at communicating or numbers? Tech or data might be calling your name. Love navigating through conversations? Politics or leadership could be your jam.

When your strengths align with what you love researching and improving, that's when magic happens. You are not just good at it—you are fulfilled by it.

5. Alright, here is the fifth sign: when you are on the right path, everything around you seems to fall in place, and the right people start showing up—maybe a mentor, a supportive friend, or even a partner who gets you.

Now, don't get me wrong—there is still effort involved. You might be working harder than ever, but the resistance from life starts to fade. It's like life is whispering. “Yes, keep going.”

6. And the last sixth sign is that every other area of your life starts to feel better too—your relationships, your health, your overall vibe—it all improves. Why? Because you are not living in conflict with yourselves anymore. You arc not chasing something out of fear or obligation. Instead, your growth feels like a celebration of your potential.

When you are aligned, you are not compensating for some void; you are stepping into your potential, and it feels like a true path, not a grind.

And here's a bonus: people around you start noticing. You might get compliments on your world without even trying. It's like the world is saying, “Yeah, you are doing exactly what you are capable of.”

So there you have it—six signs to help you know when you are on the path that's truly yours. It feels natural; you are eager to learn and update your skills, your childhood interests and your personality traits match, and life says keep going by giving support, and every other area of life falls into a better place.

Intellectually, this all might sound good. In reality, however, restlessness can be especially frustrating. They expose all kinds of hidden motivations.

Are you doing what you're doing because you are addicted to external results? Can you keep going without the constant dopamine (the feel-good neurochemical) hit that accompanies observable progress? Can you largely tune out a consumer culture trying to take you off course with endless promises of overnight success, hacks, and other enticing fads, shams, and quick fixes?

How you answer these questions is key to your ability to experience long-term success. Sometimes you need to pound the stone over and over again before it breaks. That doesn't mean your previous pounds aren't working. The tension may very well be building, and you just can't see it yet. A breakthrough might be right around the corner.

It cannot be overlooked that there are risks associated with doing the same thing that you've always done without seeing any change—whether it's in the workplace or beyond. Sometimes we spend too much time grinding it out when we'd be wiser to switch and find something more suited to our interests and skills.

Success often comes from finding the right balance between persistence and adaptability, knowing when to stay the course and when to make a change.

That knowing will come when you truly sit with yourself while knowing the difference between right and wrong. As a truest calling requires self-introspection and courage. Courage to believe in the impossible, where a world has already set a path to achieve only certain possibilities.

Boundaries

Parents were shocked, even frustrated, after learning they had turned down the unknown man's partnership. "Do you want to keep fighting lawsuits and uncertainty forever?" Their fathers are angrier than ever.

The teenagers don't have an answer to give to their parents. However, they are certain about their actions and are currently working on understanding the process.

The days blurred into one another. Orders slowed down, laughter in the kitchen faded, and the once-unstoppable trio now found themselves dragging their feet, waiting for something, anything that would point them toward their next step.

At home, the voices of their parents grew louder. Every conversation seemed to circle back to the same point:
"Stop wasting time."
"This lawsuit is proof you're not ready."
"Be practical. Do your studies."

The trio, with a sense of knowing, could feel the love in those words. But they could also feel the fear wrapped around them like chains. Fear disguised as advice. Fear disguised as protection.
The more their parents spoke, the less they could hear themselves. Their dreams, their ideas, and their quiet confidence were all drowned under a wave of mismatched beliefs.

So one evening, sitting together in their kitchen, Tara said what all three had been feeling: "I love them. We all do. But if we keep listening to their fears more than our own hearts, we will forget who we are."

Taizer nodded, his voice heavy but certain. "We are not shutting them out. But…maybe it's time to set boundaries…not to fight them, but to protect the space where our own voices can breathe…" and continued... "Should we move out? Just for a while. Maybe if we are away, things will be easier."

Tara looked at him, wide-eyed. The word "move out" carried a weight she wasn't ready for.

Taksh leaned back, staring at the ceiling. "A little silence…maybe that's what we need. To hear ourselves, without all the noise. But moving out… It's like escaping. Escaping from responsibilities isn't the answer."

He leaned forward, his tone steady and thoughtful.

"Yes, I agree, they are troubling us with their fears. Every word, every look…it feels like they don't see us. But we know the truth, don't we? Their intention isn't to hurt. It's love. Always love. Twisted by fear, yes—but still love."

He looked at both of them, his eyes shining with resolve. "So if we move out, it will hurt them as much as it hurts us. What we need are healthy boundaries. We avoid the situations where fear drowns us, but we hold on to the parts of the relationship where love is still alive. We don't stop being family; we just choose which part of the family we listen to."

Tara exhaled slowly, her lips curving into a soft smile. "So we stop fighting them. We stop trying to change them. We love them where they stand… and protect ourselves where we need to.

Taizer's shoulders eased, the weight lifting a little. "Healthy boundaries," he repeated, almost like a promise. And in that quiet kitchen, they made a pact—not to run, not to rebel, but to stand. To filter fear from love and to stay rooted in family while protecting their own dreams.

The next morning, the air at breakfast was thick, as usual. Taksh's mother spoke in a careful tone, trying not to mention the lawsuit or the future, but the tension clung to every word.
Taksh's father finally broke, "Taksh, you should just stop this kitchen nonsense now. Look at the stress it has brought."

Usually, Taksh would argue. His chest would tighten, and his words would sharpen. But this time, he paused, breathed, and simply said, "I understand, Dad." Then he left the place as if he was getting a call.

It wasn't ignorance—it was a boundary. He chose not to step into the battlefield or let fear consume the table.

Later that day, Tara found herself cornered by an aunt who said, "Bakery work is not for girls. You should be thinking about marriage." Tara smiled politely and excused herself to the kitchen. Instead of defending or exploding, she poured her energy into making tea for everyone. That was her boundary: refusing to feed into someone else's fear while still showing love in her own way.

And Taizer, when their mother tried again to push him into applying for colleges, he said calmly, "Ma, I'll think about it." Then he excused himself to review customer feedback. No yelling, no storm. Just a clean wall built where fear couldn't climb.

At night, the three met in their shared space, the kitchen table, again, their war room. They laughed about how strange it felt not to fight, to not collapse into guilt, but to stand still in their truth.

"Boundaries," Taksh whispered, holding up his glass of water like a toast.
"Love," Tara added softly, clinking her glass against his.
"And balance," Taizer finished, their three glasses touching lightly in the dim light.

Boundaries are needed in families where there is an internal and external belief mismatch, but love should be on the table. When someone is communicating their boundaries, that is them trying to keep the other person in their life, not push the other person away.

Boundaries do not mean giving up on the role of a son/daughter or not loving the parents. Boundaries are a way to create space for loving them afar, but with good intentions, where external beliefs are only valued over internal beliefs, and where expectations, assumptions, and control/force flourish instead of acknowledging the unique beliefs and circumstances of each individual.

Taksh deeply loves his parents, even in the face of their control, because he understands their intentions. Fear. And Taksh also knows it is not the only way to live.

But he cannot prove it yet. So he set healthy boundaries so as not to let those mismatched beliefs disturb his mind and started to research again about cloud kitchens.

The truth is, love between humans with unique personalities, opinions, and values under the same roof is only possible if you also stop being stubborn about your beliefs and start recognizing and embracing others' beliefs, too. And that's exactly why boundaries matter. Boundaries are not about building walls; they are about keeping relationships healthy by politely asking, “Please accept my perspective, and I will appreciate yours.”

And holding those boundaries firmly? That’s entirely on you. You are solely responsible for this.

Let me make it simple.
Say you want Italian food, but your sibling craves Chinese, and they hate Italian.
Here, you might have three choices:
1. Order separately, Italian for you and Chinese for them, and share the meal while laughing about something else.
2. Argue about it or force them, then go your separate ways, but come back the next day to chat about movies without holding onto yesterday’s disagreement.
3. Keep the grudge alive, carry it into every small conflict, and slowly let it poison the relationship

The first two choices keep relationships alive.

The last one kills them, because it’s not just about food anymore; it’s about ego.

So maybe “conditioned love” isn’t always the enemy. Maybe what you call “conditioned” is often just love trying to survive in a world of clashing perspectives. The real danger lies when you carry one hurt emotion into the next situation or moment, one disagreement into the next conversation. That’s when love stops feeling like love.
At the end of the day, relationships are meant to be lived, enjoyed, and shared.

So the next time you feel tempted to label love as conditioned or unconditional, try this instead: see it simply as love, shaped by unique perspectives and imperfect situations/moments. Blame the situation rather than the person. And remember, your perspective is as important as their perspective, too.
The trick lies in not letting one argument spill over to every part of your connection. You can have disagreements, but you also need to find spaces where you can just be happy together.

Clashes, when balanced with enough shared joy, are not a threat to a relationship; they are proof of its authenticity.

You might be thinking, "Okay, we all know this; we want to learn how to let go of grudges and move forward."

The “how” is tough, but it gets easier when you remember the root of your relationship: how innocent and joyful it once was and how life and situations got in the way.

The key is to stop letting life and situations control the relationship, and instead, let the relationship shape how you face life’s situations, even with disagreements.

When you do that, the rage softens, the grudge fades, and you can return to the relationship with joy after a disagreement and start embracing each other’s perspectives once again.

And yes, there is a limit to the number of disagreements. Learn your limits. If it's exceeded too often, perhaps it's not worth it.

Time and Patience

After realizing their true calling and setting healthy boundaries with mismatched beliefs, yet loving and being responsible teenagers to their actions and parents. Also, fighting the lawsuit and handling no-order days, the teenagers became so emotionally drained and frustrated that it showed up as rash behavior.
Handling so much that no one can see with their visible eyes made them go insane without any emotional support other than themselves.

The days began to get heavier. That was the kind of morning where even sunlight felt reluctant to enter the kitchen. The ovens were cold. The counters were clean. Too clean. There were no orders. Not a single one.

Taksh sat at the small corner desk, staring blankly at their ledger, the last few pages filled with red ink and due dates. The lawyer's payment was due in two days, and what they had left could barely cover the next batch of ingredients.
He didn't say a word. Neither did the others.

The silence in the room wasn't peace; it was pressure. The kind that makes every sound louder: the hum of the fridge, the ticking clock, and the uneven rhythm of Tara's breath.

Reality had caught up.

And it wasn't kind.

They had believed that doing it with all their heart could fix everything; the effort and good food always win. But that day, all those beliefs began to crumble.

Taizer had left earlier, hoping for a little distraction. He met an old school friend at a cafe. Someone who was now in college, relaxed, laughing, and talking about vacation plans in the mountains. It stung more than he wanted to admit.

By the time he returned to the kitchen, something inside him was already cracking.

"Did we get any orders?" he asked flatly.

Tara shook her head. "Not today either."

Taizer exhaled sharply and dropped his bag on the counter. "Of course. Why would we? Everyone else is moving forward, and we are just…stuck here cooking for ghosts."

Tara frowned. "Taizer, don't start—"

"Don't start what? Pretending this is okay?" He snapped, his voice rising. "I just met our friend; he's going on vacation with his friends and enjoying college life, and look at us! Barely scraping through lawsuits and debts."

The words burned in the air. Tara looked up, her hands trembling slightly. Something inside her, already fragile, broke too.

"You think you are the only one who's scared? She reacted back. "You think you are the only one losing sleep? You are the topper of the class, right? The smart one. Where did that smartness go in real life?

The room went still.

Her words cut deep, too deep.

Taizer froze, his face hardening. "At least without me, you wouldn't even be here. I built this business plan; I handled every order, every number, while you just ... cooked!"

Tara's eyes welled up. "And what's wrong? "That's what I love! That's what keeps this kitchen alive!"

Taksh had been silent all along, sitting at the register, staring at his phone, his father's missed calls lighting up the screen. He was already carrying his own storm from home, the same silence, the same disappointment.

He couldn't take it anymore.

"Enough!" he shouted, slamming his hand against the counter. Both of them turned to him. His voice cracked. "You want to talk about mistakes? Tara, it was your dish that caused the complaint. The lawsuit was because of you!"

The words came out before he could stop them.

Silence. A long, suffocating silence.

Tara's lips parted, but no sound came. Her tears finally fell, soft and soundless. The look on her face—it wasn't anger. It was disappointment.

Taizer glared at Taksh. "Really, Taksh? That's low—even for you."

"Low?" Taksh shot back. "I'm tired of pretending everything's fine while we are drowning!"
"Yeah?" Taizer's voice dripped with bitterness. "Says the people pleaser who can't even stand up to his dad!"

Tara left, sobbing quietly. Taizer stormed out, slamming the door so hard that the spice jars on the shelf rattled. Taksh stood there, chest heaving, realizing too late what he had said and what he couldn't take back.

The kitchen that once smelled of cinnamon and warmth now smelled like burnt air and regret.

For the first time since they began, the trio who dreamed together stood on opposite sides of the same silence.

That night was colder than usual.

Even the kitchen, their little world of warmth and laughter, felt lifeless. No sound of whisks or laughter, just the quiet hum of defeat.

Taksh sat at the dining table, head buried in his arms. The house was silent except for the faint ticking of the clock and his father's distant voice on the phone.

"Taksh," his father called from the hallway, his tone already sharp.
"Did you talk to the lawyer? What's the update on that case?"

Taksh didn't move.

His father walked closer, impatience in every step. "Are you still wasting time on that business?" One whole year—already gone! What did you even learn from this? Dreams don't feed people, Taksh!"

That last line hit something deep inside him. Something that had been buried for months—every "no," every disapproving look, every word that made him feel small, foolish, and unworthy. It all rushed like a wave too big to stop.

He stood up suddenly, eyes red, voice trembling.

"Enough, Dad!"

His father froze.

Taksh's voice cracked but didn't stop. "Enough! I have heard this every single day: that I am wasting time, that I am wrong, and that I should've just been like others. But you know what? I am tired! I am tired of proving myself every second, tired of trying to make you proud in ways that make me miserable!"
His father's face turned pale, not out of anger, but shock.

Taksh's words spilled faster, louder. "You keep saying this is for my good, that it's love—but do you even see me? I am breaking, Dad! I am scared, I am confused, but I am trying! Why is my trying never enough for you?"

The silence that followed was deafening.

His father's eyes softened for a moment, guilt flickering like a dim light, but the ego, the pride, and the fear kept him from speaking.

Taksh exhaled shakily and left the room.

He didn't slam the door. He just walked away, his legs barely carrying the weight of everything inside him.

Meanwhile, Tara sat alone in the backyard, tears streaming down her face. She had gone to check on her grandmother. She was the only person in the family who still listened without judgment.

Her grandmother placed a trembling hand on her head, brushing her hair softly.

"Why is it so hard, Grandma?" Tara said, her voice fragile. "Why do people only see failure when all we ever tried to do was something good? We didn't steal, we didn't lie, we just followed our hearts. Is that so wrong?"

Tara broke down completely. She buried her face in her grandmother's lap and sobbed—the kind of crying that doesn't ask for comfort, just release.

Her tears soaked her grandmother's dress, her shoulders shaking with months of held-in emotion—fear, guilt, anger, and exhaustion.

Her grandmother didn't say a word. She just held her with warmth and teared up a little in a way Tara cannot see.

Upstairs, in his room, Taizer sat on the edge of his bed, staring at the wall.

The fight replayed in his mind on loop: Tara's words, Taksh's voice, and his own anger. The kitchen felt miles away, but the sound of his own guilt was too close.

Each breath felt heavier than the last as he attempted to breathe. He buried his face in his hands and then cried. He cried, not the way children cry when they get hurt, but the way young adults cry when they realize life isn't fair, when effort isn't enough, when love and fear look too similar to tell apart.
He didn't want anyone to hear, pressing his face into the pillow. His chest heaved silently, his body shaking under the weight of everything he couldn't say out loud.

The next two months moved like slow rain over a windowpane—there, but barely felt.

The kitchen stayed shut.

The once-busy counters, once full of cinnamon, flour, and laughter, now gathered dust. The air that used to smell of spice and sugar smelled only of silence.

Taizer, Tara, and Taksh stopped talking about business, or dreams, or even to each other.

They weren't angry anymore—just tired.

Tired of fighting everyone, tired of explaining themselves, tired of being strong.

Their friends were posting pictures from their new colleges—hostels, campus parties. Every scroll through social media felt like another reminder of how different they were.

How "behind" they seemed.

How abnormal they looked in a world that only respects degrees and certificates.

Tara would sometimes open her recipe notebook, flip through it quietly, and close it again. Taizer buried himself in chores, pretending busyness was healing.

Taksh spent most of his time helping his mother, avoiding his father's eyes, the guilt of that night replaying like a scratch on a record.

He hadn't apologized yet, not because he didn't want to, but because he didn't know how. Every time he tried to speak, his throat closed up, the words tangled with the shame of not being a normal kid like others.

The house was quieter than ever.

Bills piled up.

The lawyer, kind enough to understand, had agreed to wait for his payment. "Sort your thing first," he said softly, seeing the defeated faces of the trio.

That kindness hurt more than any insult could have.

One evening, as the sun set behind the half-closed kitchen door, Taksh sat there alone. The shelves still had jars labeled "hope," "spice," and "love"—the same handwriting that Tara had scribbled months ago.

He touched the label "hope," and for the first time in weeks, he smiled.

A small, tired smile—but a smile nonetheless.

Because somewhere deep down, despite the silence, the guilt, and the fear, they all knew the truth:

The kitchen wasn't just a business. It was a part of them—the place where they had learned, failed, loved, and grown.

Six months passed.

Six long months since the kitchen came alive with laughter and sugar. Six months since the lawsuit drained not just their money but also their spirits.
It had been six months since the trio, once inseparable, had spoken more than a few words to each other.

Life had gone back to what everyone else called "normal."

Tara started helping her mother with housework, pretending to be okay.

Taizer spent hours scrolling job portals, feeling the weight of expectations.
Taksh… He tried to rebuild peace at home, thinking about his next step, sharing quiet dinners with his father, still carrying the guilt that had settled like dust on his heart.

Their savings were gone. The energy was gone. The fire that once defined them flickered like an ember under ash.

And yet, a small, wordless hope remained.

It showed in the way Tara was still trying to improve herself in the kitchen.
In the way, Taizer is still double-checking the old feedback forms before throwing them away.
In the meantime, Taksh still kept the kitchen key on his desk, as if he might need it again.

Then, one cold morning, as emails from colleges and lawyer bills flooded in, an email stood out.

It was from him.

The same man who had once walked into their lives with polished shoes and persuasive words.

The trio—each in their homes—read it separately.

But it felt like the same breath of wind reached all three of them at once.

Subject: "Thank you"

"Dear trio,

It's been months since our last meeting, but your story stayed with me.

You reminded me what business truly means—not power, not ownership, but creation.
Watching you defend your little dream, even in the face of overwhelming adversity, reminded me of my younger self.

I realized something: in trying to help you, I was slowly losing my own creative spark.
I was chasing safety instead of soul.

So thank you for reminding me to create, not chase.
For showing me that belief can be stronger than fear.

As business is a continuous journey of learning, I want to offer back this valuable insight, especially one that reminded me of what I had forgotten.

Amazon is hosting a competition for corporate bakeries—looking for young, creative minds to design menu experiences for multiple offices.
I have an extra ticket.
I want you three to join me.

This is not a deal. This is an opportunity—from one learner to another.

Sincerely,
The man you thought was the villain."

The email ended with a smiley—simple, human.
Tara read it twice. Then thrice. Her hands trembled as she whispered. "He…actually saw us."

Taizer leaned back in his chair, speechless, his eyes moist.

Taksh—for the first time in months—smiled without guilt.

It wasn't just about the competition. It was about being seen again—for their honesty, for their intention.

It was the universe whispering, "See? You were never wrong to believe."

That night, the air outside was cold, the kind that wrapped silence around everything.

Taizer stood inside the cold cloud kitchen, hesitant but determined. Moments later, the front door creaked again—Taksh walked in holding the printed email in his hand, folded a dozen times, edges soft from overthinking.

For a long time, they just looked at the door, like they were looking for someone else.

Taksh sighed, rubbing his forehead. "We really messed up, didn't we?

Taizer nodded, a small, defeated smile tugging at his lips.

"Yeah…badly."

The kitchen was just as they had left it—jars labeled with Tara's neat handwriting, her favorite maroon apron hanging on the hook.

The quiet hit them hard.

Taksh leaned against the counter. "I miss this place. Not the orders, not the rush…just us."

Taizer looked at him, eyes soft.

They both went silent again. Then Taksh spoke; his tone was softer now. "You know, I yelled at my dad that night. I

thought being angry would prove something. But it only showed how scared I was."
Taizer nodded.
"Same. I yelled at Tara because I was scared too—of failing, of proving everyone right. And I took it out on her again."

He looked around the kitchen once more and spoke quietly.

"We owe her more than just words."

Immediately, they went to Tara's place.

Her grandmother opened the door, gave them a knowing look, and simply said, "She's in her room."

They entered to find Tara sitting by the window, with a book open and a cup of untouched tea beside her.

She avoided looking at them, flipping a page in her book.

Okay, fair. We deserve that. Taizer winced.

Sorry, Tara. Said Taksh.

Tara didn't say anything. She kept a long pause before replying, "You both said things you didn't mean. But you know what hurt more? You didn't even check if I was okay."

Her voice trembled slightly. "You just left me hanging there, in the mess we all created."

Taizer took a step closer.

"You are right. We are cowards, Tara. I was so caught up in proving myself right, I forgot who kept us together in

the first place," he continued. "You've always been the heart of the kitchen. Without you…there's no warmth, no cinnamon, no spice."

Taksh added softly, "And no taste."

"Oh, now you remember who makes the food edible?" said Tara.

Her tone was teasing, but her eyes shimmered with tears she tried to hide.

Taizer chuckled, a soft laugh filled with relief.
"Yeah. We are hopeless without you."

Tara sighed, putting down her book. She stood and looked at both of them—two boys who had finally grown up a little.

"You are idiots," she said, crossing her arms.

Then, after a pause, "But you are my idiots."
They all laughed, the sound breaking months of silence.

Taksh held up the crumpled email. Tara looked at the email, then both.

Her lips curved into a slow, knowing smile.
"I was ready immediately after reading the mail," she said. "You two just took the scenic route to come back."

The trio sat around the old wooden table, counting the last of their earned money. Their faces were serious, but hope lingered in their eyes. After a brief discussion, they decided to borrow a small sum from their grandmother, promising her they would pay back double once the competition ended. She smiled knowingly, a twinkle in her eye, and handed them the money.

With renewed energy, they returned to their kitchen. Tara took command of the recipes, carefully measuring and experimenting with spices, fillings, and textures. Taizer handled the logistics, ensuring they had enough supplies, packaging, and presentation. Taksh coordinated taste testing, asking neighbors, friends, and family to give honest feedback to fine-tune every detail.

Weeks passed in a blur of flour, chocolate, and dedication. The scent of freshly baked pastries, vanilla, and cinnamon filled the tiny kitchen. They learned to work seamlessly, each mistake becoming a lesson, each success a small triumph.

Finally, the day of the Amazon Baker's Day competition arrived. Their stall was set up neatly, trays of muffins, croissants, and eclairs lined up with colorful labels. Employees streamed in, tasting each item and submitting their feedback on the iPad given. Excitement buzzed in the air; the trio could feel it, and even the man who offered to help them watched with pride, impressed by their persistence and dedication.

Days later, the results were announced. The trio huddled around a laptop, hearts racing. Names scrolled past, feedback poured in, and then their ranking appeared. Fifth place. Top ten, yes, but not the winner.

For a moment, the kitchen went silent. Taizer clenched his fists, Tara's hand hovered over her mouth, and Taksh leaned against the counter, unsure how to react.

Then Tara, calm as ever, smiled softly.
"We didn't win first place... But look at how far we have come. Look at what we created together. We competed honestly, with everything we had."

Taizer exhaled, a mixture of relief and pride flooding him. “She’s right; 5th place out of hundreds of competitors is not a small win at all.”

Taksh nodded, eyes bright. "And thanks to the man, we found a path we thought was closed—applying to companies looking for bakeries."

Just then, their phones rang. It was him.

“Congratulations again, trio,” the man's voice rang cheerful over the speaker. “I just checked—you made 5th place. I came in 11th myself. But don't worry, the top five will get another chance in the next few years. So this isn't the end; it's only the beginning.”

The trio exchanged glances, smiles spreading across their faces. Relief, pride, and excitement mingled in the air. 5th place was not first, but it was proof, proof that their passion, hard work, and genuine intention had carried them further than they ever imagined.

Taizer exhaled, feeling the weight lift off his shoulders.

Later, they reached out to small local cafes and offices, offering to supply pastries, snacks, and specialty baked goods. Every interaction was a lesson; some said no politely, some ignored them, and a few gave constructive feedback that sharpened their skills even further. Gradually, their network grew, one connection at a time.

Four months of persistence, countless interviews, and late-night preparations finally paid off. They received a call from the procurement office of a state university. The trio’s hearts raced as they listened. The university accepted to partner with them to supply fresh pastries and snacks for the campus cafes and events.

It wasn't just a business deal—it was validation of all their hard work, creativity, and genuine intentions. Tara's flavors, Taizer's planning, and Taksh's coordination had finally aligned into something tangible, recognized by an institution.

They celebrated quietly, knowing the journey wasn't over, but for the first time, they saw the fruits of their persistence. Every rejection, lawsuit, sleepless night, and boundary they had set had led them here.

The university deal wasn't the pinnacle—it was the doorway to a future built on intention, love, and resilience.

They even named a coupon for the man's store, promoting his business in return for gratitude for showing them a path despite their reluctance. That's true business, helping each other without taking away each other's core creativity.

Yes, there are people like the man, and you have to believe it. This is not fantasy; this is real life, where good intentions can be smelled, sensed, and rewarded. You just have to be patient enough. And patience is as messy as it will look. It's just a way of the universe making you more resilient and saying, "You deserve the best," and for that you need to level up a bit. I am trying to level you up

Patience is not always about hustling harder, chasing endlessly. It's about the space between effort and outcome. Patience consists of those idle times when nothing appears to be progressing, yet you still maintain your faith. It's the ability to stay grounded when life doesn't follow your plans, when your dreams seem distant, and when the people around you don't understand what you are waiting for.

True patience shows itself in the small, quiet battles. It's in those moments when parents question your choices, and you hold yourself out of love rather than anger. It's those nights when your heart aches from exhaustion or failure, yet you still wake up the next day and try again. It's in those lonely hours when you don't yet have the answers, but you keep searching anyway.

Patience means enduring the process of becoming without becoming bitter. We often mistake patience for passivity. We think it's weak or slow. But the truth is, patience is one of the hardest forms of strength. It demands emotional discipline. It asks us to trust that growth is happening beneath the surface, even when nothing appears to be changing.

Seeds don't bloom the moment they are planted. They take time, darkness, and stillness before they break open. The same is true for you. Your dreams and relationships all unfold in their own time. The world tells us to rush, to keep moving, to always “do something.” But sometimes, the bravest thing we can do is stand still, to allow life to shape us quietly, without forcing the outcomes.

Patience also means forgiving yourself for not being there yet, for not knowing all, for needing rest, and for feeling lost. It is giving yourself permission to grow at your own pace. In a world obsessed with speed, patience is an act of rebellion. It says, "I don't need to have it all figured out today. I just need to keep showing up.”

And in showing up—again and again with love, with effort, with gentleness—life begins to meet you halfway. You start to see that waiting was never empty. It was preparing you. Every idle moment, every tear, and every misunderstanding was shaping your character, teaching you endurance, compassion, and faith.

Practicing patience is also an important input to fulfillment. I've never met someone who described the best times of their life as "rushed."

Patience is being okay in that quiet space between effort and outcome. It's knowing you're on the right path and embracing every step of the way. Even the quiet ones.

True Success

Just before accepting the Amazon Bakers competition and rejecting the college admission his father had gotten, there was a huge scene at Taksh's home.

"This is your future, Taksh," his father said, voice sharp but shaking. "You are not going to waste your future on a mere kitchen dream. " Enough of this nonsense. You will join college next week."

Taksh's jaw tightened. "Dad, it's not nonsense. I have worked for this for almost two years. We have built something real. Please, just—"

His father slammed his hand on the table. "Real? You call that real? You call baking pastries real work? I didn't raise you for this! If you walk out of that door and reject this admission, you walk out for good."

The silence that followed cracked through the house like thunder. His mother gasped, tears brimming, "Please, don't say that…," but the words were already out, and the weight of them hung heavy in the air.

Taksh looked at his father, really looked at him, and saw not anger, but fear. That same fear he'd spent months trying to understand, trying to love through by setting healthy boundaries. But love, he realized, couldn't always mean staying silent.

He exhaled slowly. "I know you are scared, Dad. Scared that I will fail. Scared that I will waste everything you built for me. But I can't live a life that's not mine just to ease your fear."

His father turned away, jaw clenched, refusing to meet his eyes.

Taksh's voice softened. "You once told me love means wanting the best for someone. Then please…want the best for me, not the safest."

He turned, walked to his room, and began packing. His mother followed, her voice trembling.
"Taksh, please don't go. He doesn't mean it… He's just angry."
Taksh smiled weakly through his tears. "I know, Mom. He loves me. But everything has a limit—even love, when it's not understood from both sides."

He zipped his bag, and he placed a gentle kiss on his mother's forehead.

At the door, Taizer and Tara were waiting, their eyes wide with shock.

Taizer whispered, "Taksh, you said running away isn't the answer."

Taksh looked at them, eyes tired but calm. "It's not running away anymore, Taizer. It's recognizing when that love has limits. And we just need to learn our limits."

And with that, he walked into the night, not angry, not broken, but heavy with the silence of love that had reached its edge.

He started staying at a friend's apartment. The city lights outside flickered like an uncertain star—strange, distant, but still there.

One year later.

A year had passed. The trio were doing well at the university bakery. It was a living dream they nurtured with tired hands and hopeful hearts. Every day, Taizer, Tara, and Taksh poured themselves into their work, believing in themselves and what they were building.

One day, after closing hours, Taizer and Tara left together for home, laughing softly about small things. Taksh stayed back, waiting for his cab to take him to his rented room.

While standing there, his mind drifted.

Earlier that day, he had seen a father come to pick up his son from campus. It wasn't a rare sight—every day he saw something similar. Sometimes a mother waiting patiently, sometimes a father smiling proudly. Scenes so ordinary for others, yet painfully loud for him.

He didn't realize when his eyes got wet. The cab arrived. Taksh took the window seat and stared outside as the city lights blurred past him. His thoughts ran faster than the cab.

Somewhere deep inside, guilt tightened its grip again.

If only I were normal.
If only I had gone to college.

He imagined his father's happiness—the pride in his eyes if Taksh had chosen the so-called "right" path. Taksh wanted that happiness for him. He wanted to be a son his parents could proudly talk about.

But the thought faded as quickly as it came. "I'm not worthy of that pride anyway," he said to himself.

This guilt had been living with him for days, growing heavier with time. Taizer and Tara noticed it clearly. The spark Taksh once carried—his confidence, his warmth—had dimmed. He had begun to see himself as a bad child, someone who hurt his parents simply by being himself.

Yet, despite everything, he never doubted his work.
He knew he was capable.
He knew this path was his calling.

What he lacked wasn't belief in himself—but belief from his parents. And that absence turned into guilt. He carried their disappointment on his shoulders instead of their love. His shoulders often clenched, as if holding a weight that wasn't meant to be his.

He stopped being himself as he once did. He stopped encouraging others. Somewhere along the way, he convinced himself he had no right to encourage others.

Life became mechanical—work, eat, sleep. No laughter. No spark.

His work gave him an unknown courage. But his parents' rejection slowly took away his confidence.

One day, the university invited Zen Buddhists to speak to students about life. The trio received invitations too. Taizer and Tara attended eagerly—and dragged Taksh along with them.

He listened quietly to all the talk. After a while, he became restless. Enough of this gyaan, he thought. "Life has already taught me more than enough through pain," he said to himself.

He decided to leave and head to the cafe to work.

Just then, the final speech began.

A voice asked, "What will be your immediate thought after knowing that the most successful person went through insane challenges and pain to reach the top?"

Taksh stopped mid-step. Something made him turn around.

The question echoed again, and he looked back to see who had asked it.

It was a girl. A simple moment—but powerful enough to make him pause. He had never felt that way before. It was unfamiliar and unexplainable.
She repeated the question. "What will be your immediate thought after knowing that the most successful person went through insane challenges and pain to reach the top?"

A student from the crowd answered loudly, "Wow! So great! Such an inspiration!"

The girl smiled gently.

"Yes—exactly," she said.
"If you find inspiration and strength from someone else's struggles, then tell me—who will be your cheerleader for your journey?" she asked.

Silence fell.

"Self-love," she continued, "for walking your self-made creative path. And self-kindness—for every challenge you've faced and every effort you've made."

She paused, then said softly, "You deserve self-love too."

She then ended with a simple, "Thank you all. Please be careful in the crowd."

Taksh stood there, unmoving. For the first time in a long while, something inside him loosened.

Most of the time, in the process of becoming a responsible child, a responsible member of society, and someone who constantly balances work and emotional expectations, you slowly forget one thing—to love yourself.

While trying to meet responsibilities, society and its deeply rooted beliefs often whisper that you are not enough—especially when you choose to create a new path, a path that doesn't fit into the familiar old measuring scale.

That very measuring scale—the one used to compare, judge, and define success—can make the journey painfully lonely. And it is exactly at this point, when you feel most alone, that self-respect becomes essential. Respecting your journey and your courage is crucial.

This path teaches a quiet but powerful truth: Nothing external is permanent. Approval changes. Opinions shift. Validation depends on the measuring tape of the moment. What is praised today may be questioned tomorrow.

The only thing that truly remains is self-love.
Love for your efforts.
Love for your journey.
Love for the courage it takes to walk your own path.

Self-love does not mean rebellion. It exists alongside respect—for your parents, for society, and for the world around you. But it also teaches you an important boundary: You are not responsible for someone else's internal struggles, wounds, fears, insecurities, or disappointments that arise from their own measuring tape.

You are responsible only for your effort, your integrity, and your intent.

Self-love is gentle. It means appreciating yourself when no one is clapping. It is empathizing with yourself when things feel heavy. Self-love involves listening to your inner voice rather than silencing it.

Self-love is also about keeping promises—to yourself. Because every small promise you break slowly erodes your self-respect. And every promise you keep builds trust within. Just like any meaningful relationship, the one with yourself also needs trust, loyalty, honesty, and respect. Just don't abandon yourself when things get difficult, and don't belittle yourself for choosing differently. You just be.

And when you do that—when you walk your path with the right intention and the right effort with courage, self-love, and self-kindness while being a responsible being to your surroundings—that is true success.

Peace

The house felt different without Taksh—quieter, emptier. The chair he used to drag across the table sat untouched. The kitchen, once filled with his late-night experiments and laughter, now smelled only of silence.

His father buried himself in work. Every evening, he came home to the same stillness, to the same empty chair. He never said it aloud, but every night, his eyes lingered on that empty space a little longer.

One night, while checking his emails after dinner, he noticed something unexpected—a newspaper article forwarded by a colleague.

It read:
"Three teenagers win local recognition for innovative home bakery model—cloud kitchen dreamers bring heart to the food business."

There was a photo—Tara holding a tray of pastries, Taizer flashing a proud grin, and Taksh…standing behind them, smiling softly, sleeves rolled up, flour on his cheek.

His father froze. His breath caught somewhere between pride and disbelief. For a moment, he stared at the article, eyes tracing his son's name—the same name he once scolded, doubted, and dismissed. But he quickly shrugged it off, pretending it wasn't serious. "It's just a small local thing," he muttered, setting the newspaper aside.

The following holiday season, his wife gently insisted, "You should call him. It's been months." But his pride—or whatever shield he had built around himself—wouldn't let him.

Then one quiet morning, as he flipped through the paper, something caught his eye.
A headline read:
"Eighteen-year-old wins world chess championship—drops out of school to follow his passion."

He stared at it for a long time. Something inside him cracked—not in anger, but in pain. That article didn't just speak about a boy; it spoke to him. It reflected everything he had refused to see—that success doesn't have one form, one formula, or one path.

The ache deepened as he thought of his son—of Taksh's determination, his sleepless nights, and his quiet resilience in the face of rejection and fear. And suddenly, it hurt. It hurt to realize that he, who prided himself on being a provider and protector, had become the very reason his son had to fight.

It taught him that there is never only one way to succeed. That people carry different dreams, and each dream comes with its own truth, its own risk, and its own light. And that he must learn to respect those unique choices, even when they seem uncertain, even when they don't fit the world's mold.

He realized something profound that day:
"Only when a person takes the first step does he begin to see the view of where he is going. Until then, the road will always look uncertain. But taking that first step—that takes courage."

And for the first time, he saw his son clearly—not as a rebel or a disappointment, but as someone who had the courage to take that step when even he, a grown man, could not.

Taksh's father felt proud—not of the business they were running, not of their sales or recognition, but of their bravery. Of the way those teenagers stood tall despite disagreement, loneliness, and fear.

He realized something else too, something that stayed with him like a quiet truth:
Parents should be ready to support their children's choices—because they brought them into this world. But the world, including himself, had reversed that—expecting children to support their parents' fears instead of their own dreams.
For the first time in years, he saw his own immaturity reflected in his child's calm maturity.

And in that moment, he didn't just feel proud. He felt humbled.

Taksh's mother noticed her husband sitting alone at the dining table, the newspaper still open to that same article. His tea had gone cold.
She didn't say anything. She just placed her hand on his shoulder—a quiet nudge that said it's time.
He didn't resist this time. He simply nodded, stood up, and took his coat.

Taksh sat at the back of the university bakery, his laptop open in front of him, the screen glowing with unfinished work. Around him, voices overlapped—but his mind was far away.

Her words kept replaying on a quiet loop.

He stared at the cursor blinking on the screen, but instead of ideas, memories surfaced. The weight he had been carrying for so long—guilt, shame, the constant feeling of being a disappointment—felt exposed, as if someone had gently named it out loud for the first time.

Then, while Taksh's eyes quietly wandered over the crowd of students, he saw a familiar figure at the entrance—hesitant, scanning the tables.

It's his father.

For a moment, Taksh froze. It had been a year since he had seen him. The last memory he had was of raised voices and the sound of a suitcase zipping shut. Now, his father stood there, older somehow—or maybe just quieter.

When their eyes met, something heavy lifted between them. They sat in silence for a while, watching the university students drift in and out.

After a long pause, his father spoke—almost to himself.

"Look around you, Taksh."
Taksh followed his gaze.
"These teenagers," his father said, "none of them really know anything yet. They are all trying to understand the same way you are. The same way I still am."
Taksh looked at him, surprised.
His father continued, his tone gentle and raw:
"I used to think being a parent meant having all the answers. If I could make you follow the safe path, I'd be protecting you from mistakes. But now I see…maybe I was just protecting myself from fear. Fear of you failing. Fear of being wrong. Fear that I would not fit in society."
Taksh's eyes softened. "Dad…"
His father shook his head, eyes glistening.
"You were right to follow what you believed in. I see it now. You have learned what no classroom could have

taught you—not from grades nor from books, but from life itself."
The words touched Taksh like warmth after a long winter.

He leaned forward, his voice trembling. "I am sorry too, Dad. For the words I said…for walking out. I just couldn't keep proving myself anymore."

His father smiled—a tired, genuine smile. "You don't have to anymore."

They sat there in quiet understanding. No grand apology, no dramatic gestures—just two people who had finally seen through each other's fear.

Taksh looked around again—at the students—and this time, he didn't feel behind.

He felt free.
And with freedom, peace accompanied, naturally.

Intangible Wealth

To be honest, life didn't suddenly become easy for the trio.

They were still paying bills, the lawyer fees for the ongoing food-poisoning case that never should have existed in the first place, just for choosing purity: real, fresh food. Bread made from scratch, milk sourced directly from farms, not factories. Food made with care, not shortcuts, unlike fast-food chains.

It wasn't their food that paused them. It was because of those guts that got used to artificial convenience that reacted to something real.

Yet, despite knowing they weren't at fault, they paid the price and still are paying.

Did those bills stop them? Yes. They slowed them down, made them question, and forced them to pause, only to help them reach full clarity, only to know without doubt that this was their true calling. And when that certainty arrived, they stood back up—stronger than before.

In that whole process, the trio gained wealth that could never be taxed, stolen, or sued.
They gained wisdom, the ability to survive in a world full of mismatched beliefs...an intangible wealth.
They gained bonding, their relationships strengthened by shared storms...an intangible wealth.
They gained skills, earned through relentless effort...an intangible wealth.
They gained courage, the courage to embrace their uniqueness, while being able to differentiate right from wrong, even when it cost them... an intangible wealth.

And slowly, quietly, the tangible wealth followed.

Money began reaching heights like no other teenager their age was touching—not by luck, not by noise, but in direct proportion to the effort they invested, while balancing effort with right intention, ambition with integrity, and growth with respect for every relationship they carried.

They weren't brave because they were fearless.
They were brave because they believed in their purity.

It was never about age. Never about timing. Never about who was watching or who wasn't.

It's only about showing up for your pure core self, even when there is no support, no applause, and no visible result yet.

Taksh meets Zyda.

Taksh finally found her.

The girl who had made him stop mid-step.
The girl who had unknowingly turned his gaze to look inward. After months of struggle, he finally got to know her name—Zyda. She stayed in the university dorms. That much he knew. And strangely, that was all he knew. She never came to their bakery. And he is not a student of the university. Their worlds barely overlapped. The only thread connecting them was that Zen Buddha session, the one he had almost walked out of, dismissing it as too much gyaan. He still believed he wasn't as deep or as philosophical as her. Yet his heart betrayed logic; it pulled him toward her with a quiet insistence he couldn't explain.

So one random day, acting more on impulse than courage, he decided to check on her. He asked Tara for help; she knew a girl in the dorms. With her assistance, Taksh found himself walking down a narrow dormitory corridor, his heartbeat loud in his ears.

As he approached Zyda's room, the door suddenly opened.

A girl stormed out, crying uncontrollably, her face red, her voice sharp with rage.
*"She's a bi***,", the girl screamed, wiping her tears. "Stay away from her!" The girl brushed past him, still cursing, her footsteps echoing down the hallway.*

Frozen for a moment, Taksh didn't realize he had already crossed the threshold.

He was inside the room.

Zyda's room. The door clicked shut behind him.

Nervousness crept over him like never before. He didn't know where to stand or whether he should even be there. His eyes wandered instinctively around the room, beautifully arranged, calm, and perfect. Plants by the window. Books stacked neatly. A quiet order that felt intentional.

Then he saw it.

Blood. A dark smear on the rim of a plant pot.

His breath caught.

On the side table lay a book—a vampire book. And resting on it was a fingernail. The fingernail was completely torn off. Fresh. Bloody.

His heart pounded as he leaned closer, confusion overtaking fear.
Before he could process it—"Did you finish all the checking?"

Her voice.

Taksh flinched and turned around sharply.

Zyda stood there, calm, unreadable, her gaze steady on him.

For a moment, he forgot how to breathe.

He pointed awkwardly toward the door.
"The girl… She was crying. She was cursing you. Why?"

"Because she hates herself," Zyda replied, her tone serious, almost detached.

Taksh swallowed. "And…that blood—"

Before he could finish, Zyda interrupted, her voice firm now.

"Who are you? And why are you in my dorm room?"

The question hit him harder than anything. He searched for an answer but found none.

"I…I don't know," he said honestly. "You made me come here."

"What?" Zyda asked, genuinely confused.

He shook his head quickly. "Nothing. I'll meet you again."

Without waiting for a response, Taksh turned and left, his steps hurried, his thoughts tangled, and his heart racing.

He didn't know what frightened him more:
What he had seen in that room…
Or the girl who had quietly, inexplicably taken his heart.

While he was walking back to bakery, he realized one thing was certain—

Zyda is not just a mystery.

She is a kind of magic—quiet, rare, and waiting to be understood.

And without fully knowing why, Taksh wanted to be part of that magic.

Part 2 is where the magic begins!